AGAINST ALL ODDS

Front cover (top): David in Class 2, 2nd Floor, Carlson House School.

Front cover (bottom): Pupils and Staff at Carlson House School c. 1953. Anthony and David are seated together, on the far right of the third row. Maureen is seated 4th from the right, on the front row.

Back cover: David & Maureen on the balcony of their Hotel, in Corfu, 1988.

AGAINST ALL ODDS

The Carlson House Legacy

David Barnsley &
Shirley Thompson

BREWIN BOOKS

BREWIN BOOKS
56 Alcester Road,
Studley,
Warwickshire,
B80 7LG
www.brewinbooks.com

Published by Brewin Books 2018

A CIP catalogue record for this book is available from the
British Library.

ISBN: 978-1-85858-564-2

Printed and bound in Great Britain
by 4edge Ltd.

Contents

Acknowledgements

The authors are indebted to the following people, companies and organisations, for their invaluable contributions, various favours and support, which have been of great assistance in the publication of this book.

Our special thanks to Anna Southall, (Paul Cadbury's eldest granddaughter) for an inspired *Foreword*.
The Barrow Cadbury Trust.
Friends/Carers (also includes majority of those listed below – and under other headings): Raj Bartlett; Vera Dean – (Swiss holiday); Mary and John Fletcher; Jane Hall; Joe McGuire; Roger Robinson; Jenny and Pete Willock.
Physiotherapist/ Health Advisor: Tina Hackett
Queen Elizabeth Hospital: Doctor Shyam Madathil, Consultant Respiratory Physician; team of nurses: Jody, Theresa and Lyndsey.

Companies and Associations:
Birmingham Post and Mail – see Bibliography
Cerebral Palsy West Midlands: Gary Watson – Manager; Barbara Brand – Senior Social Worker.
Disability Resource Centre, Birmingham: Pete Millington (particular thanks for his Disability Timeline).
Hanover Housing Association Extra Care Development – three facilities:
a) Dave Barnsley's place of residence; b) Mears Care Staff: including Abdul, Aisha, Rabina and Salim; **c) Two separate teams:** Day Nurses under the leadership of Marie; Night Nurses: (available if needed).
Publishers: Alan and Alistair Brewin of Brewin Books Ltd.
Staff and Associates of the Westley Hotel, Acocks Green: Alex Powell; staff members: Lyn and the manager – Kieran.
Websites (various): see Bibliography.

Gretty. BY KIND PERMISSION OF
CEREBRAL PALSY MIDLANDS.

Foreword

This moving account of David's life starts at home. Aged six, in 1947 David was offered a place at the newly founded Carlson House School in Birmingham, giving him a start that he has described as the catalyst that enabled him to lead a productive and full life. The funding for this ground-breaking school came from the Ministry of Health and Education, matched by funding from Paul Cadbury, the Birmingham Quaker and business man, my grandfather. Inspired by his own experience and observations, and by the success of the school over a quarter of a century, the Paul S Cadbury Trust invested in further facilities in 1970, and remained a significant funder until the school's closure in 1982.

Paul and Rachel Cadbury lived in Birmingham; Henrietta Margaret, known to her family as Gretty, was the youngest of their five children and was diagnosed at birth with cerebral palsy. Perhaps unusually for those times, Paul and Rachel had no hesitation in looking after her at home. The house was adapted to accommodate Gretty's mobility needs, and the family were helped by a dedicated team of carers. So determined were her parents that she should be treated no differently from the other children that Gretty's two youngest siblings often recalled going to bed still hungry, having been given supper with Gretty in the nursery at an age when they might reasonably have expected to join their parents and older siblings downstairs for dinner.

Gretty died aged twenty in 1950 when I, her oldest niece, was only two. I thus have no personal memory of her. However, her life had a deep impact on all her family, even those unborn at the time of her early death. Two of her siblings chose careers in medicine. Perhaps more profoundly, all four of them had a far greater understanding not only of the needs but, equally importantly, the possibilities in life for young people overcoming the challenges of cerebral palsy.

This is something that they shared within their own families, enabling us all as able-bodied members of an inclusive society to relate to those with a disability. Through our service as trustees, Gretty's legacy has been a very important influence on the Barrow Cadbury Trust's charitable giving and focus on equalities for 60 or more years.

In a letter to my grandfather following Gretty's death, Sir Leonard G Parsons, the distinguished Birmingham paediatrician, reflected those feelings. He wrote of:

> '...the wonderful things that have come out of her life, not in spite of but because of her disabilities. Had she not lived there would have been no Carlson House in Birmingham, and no brightness of life or achievement for crippled children. It is true that she was wonderfully blessed in her parents, but even they might never have thought of this great work without her inspiration. She could certainly say that she had done the work that was given her to do, and that many children's lives have been made so much happier and worthwhile because of her.'

Shirley Thompson's account makes a moving biography. David's anecdotes of the ups and downs of life at home, work and on holiday, and of lifelong friendships formed at Carlson House School, give us an uplifting insight into what life has been like for him, and for so many with a disability, over the last 77 years. Much of the support given by institutions like Carlson House is now of course provided by the public, voluntary or social enterprise sector and there can be no doubt that huge advances have been made in perceptions, enablement and support. But this progress, and any continuing improvements for those with a disability, can by no means be taken for granted in this era of austerity and cuts.

The nurturing and supportive environment of Carlson House provided succour and stability in David's youth, and a very precious opportunity to nurture some invaluable lifelong friendships. His indomitable spirit has obviously helped him face the adversities life has presented to him. But, above all, it is David's 'can do' attitude that will be an inspiration for anyone living with a disability.

Anna Southall
August 2017

Prologue

Dear Reader,

I'd like to tell you a little bit about my life and times.

When a beautiful bouncing baby was born prematurely, on 13th August 1941, to his proud parents, Jessie and Ronald Barnsley, little did they realise the problems that lay ahead.

It was only as the days turned into weeks and the weeks turned into months… and the months turned into years… that the full extent of my handicap became apparent.

I failed to develop, from crawling to walking and it became obvious to my parents that there was something seriously wrong.

They took me to a Specialist – who didn't help either – as he stated: "There's nothing wrong with the boy. Bring him back when he walks!" As I never did, I never went back to him.

It is the sincerest hope of both myself and my Biographer, Shirley Thompson that, as my story unfolds, it will provide some degree of insight, into what life has been like for those of us with a disability, over the past seventy-seven years.

With many good wishes,

Dave Barnsley

David Barnsley

Anthony Hugh Sutton.

DEDICATION

This book is dedicated to 'mon ami mate',
Anthony Hugh Sutton, MBE, BA (Hons).
We shared life's 'ups-and-downs' together.

This Ability

'Tis a universally-acknowledged fact –
A 'Given', if you please
That each of us, at birth,
Is given diverse abilities.

But if we are born handicapped
In Movement, Speech or Sight,
We have to labour doubly hard
To make our future right.

No fame or fortune wait for us
For we haven't had a choice
But with courage, hope and love we strive,
To find that special voice.

Our Psyche may be wounded
By trauma you cannot see
Emotions locked away inside
May hide the real Me.

So if in wheelchair I pass by
Autistic, deaf or blind
Please don't assume I have no heart
I'm reaching out – be kind.

In my dreams I'm soaring to the clouds
Above all worldly strife.
Please talk to me – not my Carer
For I, also, seek a life.

© Shirley Thompson 2018

Chapter One

1941 – 1947
Bring Him Back
When He Walks!

11 August 1941 was a momentous day. Winston Churchill and F.D. Roosevelt met on a ship off Newfoundland (now part of Canada) to sign the Atlantic Charter, which condemned territorial changes and affirmed human rights.

Two days later, a young baby boy was brought into this world, but such was his predicament, every day was destined to be a struggle, simply to maintain his own human rights! That same year, Noel Coward's 'Blythe Spirit' was performed for the very first time, Bob Dylan was born; James Joyce, Amy Johnson and Virginia Woolf died.

'Big Boy', thought to be the biggest steam locomotive ever built, went into service for the Union Pacific railroad company in the USA. You'll be hearing that name again shortly, but in a totally different context!

In December 1941, as our baby slept innocently in his cradle, the Japanese made a surprise air attack on the US naval base at Pearl Harbor; eight battleships and over 300 aircraft were either destroyed or damaged.

77 years later, the child in question is about to tell you his story...

I was born on 13 August, 1941. The first thing I remember is a wheelchair... I liked it so much I never got out of it! I was born in Hazlewell Nursing Home, Kings Heath, just around the corner from here. We lived at 66 Pakefield Road, Kings Norton, Birmingham 30. It was an ordinary house, so at night I had to go upstairs on my bottom, into my bedroom and up onto the bed. My mother, Jessie, gave me a bath once a week. My father made something I could climb onto and

David Barnsley's parents' wedding: 9.30am, August 27, 1938. Jessie Winifred Mustin and Ron Barnsley (H.R.). Back row, l-r: Grandma and Granddad Barnsley; Best Man, Alf Barnsley (brother); the bride and groom; Granddad (Joseph) and Nanny Mustin. Bridesmaids: left – Rosemary Whetnal; right – chief bridesmaid: Ethel Mustin (sister). Kings Norton Methodist Church, Birmingham.

then into the bath. I came down the same way in the morning, shuffling along on my bottom! My mother cooked all of my meals for me. She never went out to work; she looked after me.

My memories go back to around the age of three. I remember having leg calipers and I could walk along a blank wall, or with assistance. But I was carried for much of the time, by my father, when we went out in the car.

My father had an Austin Ruby pre-war car. We'd sometimes collect my Grandfather Barnsley, from 215 Selly Oak Road and take him for a little run.

I remember Grandfather, sitting in the Front Room at 215, with his brass bedstead, a bowl and pitcher. He'd be sitting in a chair, exercising his left hand all the time. I was very young at the time, but he'd had a stroke. He passed away in 1948.

My father worked for *George H. Hughes*, which was in Edgemond Avenue, Tyburn. They made spoked wheels for wheelchairs and things like that – which became quite useful! He was able to get me a pushchair, which also had a leg-rest; at that time I could straighten my legs.

I went into hospital in about 1944 – Grandfather probably paid for that. He had a Nursery up at Brandwood End. He supplied the money, because it was

David's Birth Certificate.

before the National Health Service. I knew I was disabled, but my parents seemed to always have this feeling that I would get better:

"In every way, in every day, you feel a little bit better," is what they used to say. Although I never really got on with my father, because he was always putting me down, telling me that I had big ears and that I was goofy, because my teeth stuck out.

I didn't like it at the time, but I realise now why he did it... possibly... being more charitable in my old age. It *may* have been reverse psychology, to make me more determined.

I craved his affection all my life – but I never got it. I wanted a bit of praise, but I never got that either. He was second generation Victorian, so of course, you didn't show your emotions! However, I learned things about my father quite recently, which I never knew about before. I was brought up by both parents, to believe that I was the result of their love for each other.

In 1944 I went into the Woodlands Orthopaedic Hospital, to have my feet manipulated. Mr Hughes was my surgeon. We only saw our parents once a fortnight. I'd be about three at that time.

My mother told me that it was all right, because they didn't bomb hospitals. What she *hadn't* told me was that they'd already bombed the hospital and damaged the tower! As soon as there was any fresh air, you were wheeled out. I was a very pernickety eater, so they used to leave the food out until either you or the flies had eaten it – and the flies usually won! Mummies and Daddies came once a fortnight. When we saw them coming we used to chant:

"Mummies and Daddies are coming today, Mummies and Daddies are coming today." They stayed the magnificent time of an hour, every fortnight.

I wasn't in there for very long, although in those days a large majority of people were in for years! I had these operations and it was rather interesting that if your parents went to see a specialist it would be a case of:

"Well we could do this for you, but it's up to you. Make up your mind, or I don't want to see you again!" So there was a bit of a veiled threat underlying that.

I used to dread going to Broad Street, which was the Outpatients Department of the Orthopaedic Hospital. The building is still there, but it's a hotel now, I believe.

Baby Dave. Photographer Roy Dixon.

I was brought up in a very cosseted world, so I believed everything that my parents told me. It eventually became clear that there were other people with my disability. Originally it was called 'Infantile Paralysis'.

I started school when I was around five or six years old. That was George Street West. We were picked up by a single-decker municipal bus, which caused quite a stir as it drove up the road. There was a lady on there, who helped you on. I sat on the front seat and started to meet the people. The school isn't there now; it was off Five Ways, on the Ladywood side.

George Street West was a multi-handicapped school. I walked about, pushing a chair, which meant that I was bent over. I was told to stand up straight and use the back of the chair, but when I did that, I fell over! So I took no notice of that. I was afraid of being sent to the Head, to be caned

They probably wouldn't have caned handicapped children, but I *thought* they would; and being a multi-handicapped school, I was always afraid of being left behind. So I used to push my chair out into the playground, ready for the bus. But I was told off, because when it rained, the chairs got wet.

I was the sort of child who always did as he was told. I was also very nervous: I lived off my nerves... and I still do!

During one of my hospital stays, a Miss Woodall came to see me, and talk to me about things in general. She decided that I had enough intelligence to be considered for Carlson House for Spastics, which was in its infancy. It was named after a guy who had founded similar schools in America.

Going back to George Street West, one of the passengers was Peter Davis, who always wet himself. As the water dripped through the seat onto the floor it produced what we called him – 'Puddle'!

There was a girl on the seat behind me, called Beryl Speake: whatever you said to her, she answered in rhyme! At the back of the bus were two brothers, Ken and Brian Powell; they were the big boys. The reason why I mention these people is that I came across them, later in life. Ken and Brian had another brother who died. All three brothers were what came to be known as 'spastic'... all in the same family.

It's not a genetic condition at all, it's to do with the birth – starvation of oxygen – although my mother swore to the day she died that she didn't know what had caused *me* to be the way I was.

The thing that has always been a big problem in our lives is Transportation. My father worked most of the time, but he had a car. It was quite a journey for him, to go from Kings Norton to Tyburn, on a daily basis. That's nothing now, but it was quite a big journey then. The car was unreliable and he used to try to repair it himself.

I don't know what he did when his car broke down. I remember the trams going up the middle of the Bristol Road – I went on one once.

My Grandfather also had a car, so I'd go out with him in his Austin, registration number COP 4. That was my mother's father, who owned the Nursery. He delivered tomatoes, for sale in shops, which I remember vividly: he was a terrible driver! I'd sit in the front passenger seat beside him; I wasn't in a wheelchair at that stage.

Nowadays children sometimes use their mother's name, but in those days she was just 'mother' to me. I never dreamt of calling my father Ron, which was the name he used – or Jessie. If they had a row they went upstairs, so that they wouldn't disturb me. I knew when my father was in a bad mood – but that's another story. I remember him working Saturday mornings, then coming back at one o'clock.

They always had a dog, but the first dog, as soon as I arrived, disappeared for six weeks. It was a Scottish Terrier – Kim. Then it suddenly reappeared... they had no idea where it had been! They had Springer Spaniels after that.

Until I was sixteen I went to bed at seven o'clock every night, which was detrimental to me in later years, because I couldn't keep awake. Now I can't keep awake for other reasons. I used to listen to the kids playing outside – and I was in bed – resting – supposedly! I wanted to be outside with them, but you see, I was different. Kids especially looked at me aghast! They either stared... and got a slap from their parents or, as in later years, as a defence mechanism. I'd look

Ethel's 80th Birthday Party, at a Golf Club, just outside Stratford-upon-Avon. From l-r: Jessie, Ethel and Madge.

them straight in the eye and say, "Take a good look – you might never see me again!" and hope for the best.

My parents weren't well off. My father gave my mother Housekeeping, which was a bit of a problem at times... He didn't like things going up!

He was a Chartered Company Secretary and could add up a line of figures, in his head. He worked at *George H Hughes* for quite a long time. I used to go on a Saturday morning and open the post. Then I got too heavy for him to carry me up the stairs. Steps and stairs were a really big problem for me.

In July 1948 I left George Street West, at the age of seven. A new, highly significant, eleven-year experience was about to begin for me, when I became a pupil at the newly-opened, groundbreaking, Carlson House School for Spastics, in September of that year.

Chapter Two

1930 – 1974
From Carlson House to Long John Silver

Since it started in 1947 this has been one of the outstanding success stories in the treatment of handicapped children. It is still a very happy ship. Recently we have been considering whether we could install a new classroom specially designed for the older severely handicapped children, where they could have a certain amount of independence. The result is a unique lay-out. In addition we propose to add on a new classroom for 5-to-6-year-olds, so that the present large room can be used as a school hall…

Paul Cadbury, 28 January 1970: extract from a letter to fellow trustees, of the Paul S. Cadbury Trust.

(*A History of the Barrow Cadbury Trust*, p76: Merlin Waterson and Samantha Wyndham).

Paul Cadbury's youngest child, Henrietta Margaret, known to her family as 'Gretty', was born with cerebral palsy, in 1930. It was Henrietta Margaret's condition that prompted her father to establish Carlson House in Birmingham in 1947.

During a visit to the States in 1946 Paul Cadbury had met Earl Carlson – and his inspirational idea began to take shape.

Sadly, Margaret died in 1950, at the age of twenty, but during her lifetime her parents, Rachel and Paul, looked after her at home, assisted by a team of Carers. They rarely left her on her own and took separate holidays, to ensure that someone was always with her.

Paul and Rachel Cadbury's children, in 1933, from l-r: Henrietta Margaret ('Gretty'), Catherine, Edward, Charles and Philippa (Anna Southall's mother – see Foreword). BY KIND PERMISSION OF CEREBRAL PALSY MIDLANDS.

Paul had originally planned a career in medicine, but this was interrupted by the war. However, 'Gretty's' condition seems to have had a significant influence on the lives of some of her older siblings: Catherine married a consultant surgeon; Phillipa, Anna Southall's mother, read medicine at Birmingham University and Edward became a doctor.

Paul Cadbury's granddaughter, Anna, explains so eloquently, in her *Foreword* to our book, how 'Gretty's' diagnosis at birth, profoundly affected the lives of many other children, with cerebral palsy.

David Barnsley now returns as Narrator, for the remainder of our book. The words of any other contributors to the book are shown within speech marks.

* * * * *

From the age of six, I was one of the first children from the Birmingham area to attend a pioneering new school for children with cerebral palsy, called Carlson House in Harborne, Birmingham. It was a centre of excellence set up with the support of Birmingham's well known Cadbury family.

At the end of the war, Paul Cadbury was visiting America on Business when he learnt of the theories of Doctor Earl Carlson. Doctor Carlson had cerebral palsy himself and he had written a book stating his views that children with cerebral palsy were educable.

Paul Cadbury gathered together a group of people who were prepared to support his venture and to give it some finance. People like Ken Quayle of Quayle Carpets in Kidderminster and others and they also gained the interest of Birmingham Education Department, who agreed to put up some money.

They purchased a large house at 13A Victoria Road, in Harborne, which had a large garden and stables and from 1945 the building was made suitable for the education of children with cerebral palsy.

The school was partly funded by the Ministry of Health and Education, but the other half of all the capital costs was financed by the Paul S. Cadbury Trust.

The Founders of Carlson House School. From l-r: Stephen Quayle, Ilse Carlson, Earl Carlson and Paul Cadbury. BY KIND PERMISSION OF CEREBRAL PALSY MIDLANDS.

In those days parents didn't get grants so they banded together with other parents. I recall going as a child of about 5 or 6 to 13A Victoria Road for weekends where my parents helped with working parties who were converting the house.

I recall that there was a *Covered Way* from the house to the stables, with 17 windows along the side, which gives you some idea of the size of the area that was converted into the physiotherapy department. This is where physiotherapy and speech therapy were offered on a daily basis.

On the 8 September 1948, Carlson House opened its doors to its first group of pupils. I feel a great sense of debt towards the staff and everyone else involved with Carlson House, in those early days.

The first headmistress was Miss Christine Woodall, a kind lady. She became Mrs Brown, but later on she went away to work at Ponds, which belonged to the Spastic Society. I kept in touch with her and she came to my 60th birthday.

The criteria set for admission to Carlson House was based on a certain IQ level and children were vetted to see if they would benefit from what was offered.

I recall that the kids used to be collected each morning by pre-war Austin taxis supplied by the All-Electric Garage in Harborne – they were dubious vintage; even the journey from home was exciting because of the tendency for the vehicles to break down at least every seven days. The spare car came to pick you up and then that would break down too – we'd have the back number plate in the boot as we arrived at school. It was a precarious choice between which car was most broken down!

The cars became symbols; we were attached to them and recalled them by their registration plates. There was 'Ada', 'Ea' and, rather sophisticated, a pre-war Armstrong Siddeley, with an unfortunate number plate reading 'CAC'! And that is how we got to school.

On the first day, one of the occupants, Peter Davis, was sick over the driver's lunch! Peter was in the bed next to me, when I was at the Children's Hospital.

We arrived to be taken by physios to be assessed. Whenever we were taken from the classrooms to therapy sessions, orderlies would wheel us away in chairs, adapted with wheels on the back, which had been provided by a local antique dealer, Mr Howell; as you grew they would come along and alter the chairs. A highlight of life at Carlson House was in 1955 when Roy Rogers visited the school; he was over in Birmingham with Trigger and his wife, Dale Evans. Carl Chinn later told me that Roy had been appearing at the Birmingham Hippodrome at that time.

Richard Hearne, 'Mr Pastry', also visited the school. He was prepared to put in a swimming pool, but the idea was rejected, possibly due to maintenance and staffing costs.

My parents and I went with a working party on Saturday afternoons, to help adapt the building, which was Victorian.

I remember playing with mini-bricks at the Harborne school, which were rubber bricks, before Lego. One of the pupils' fathers made a beautiful doll's house... Derick Green's father. Derick was a similar age to myself.

With these working parties, people gathered together – that was all we had really. We started to gather at a church in Lyndon Road, Cotteridge and to see old films: Charlie Chaplin and that sort of thing. I'd be about six at the time.

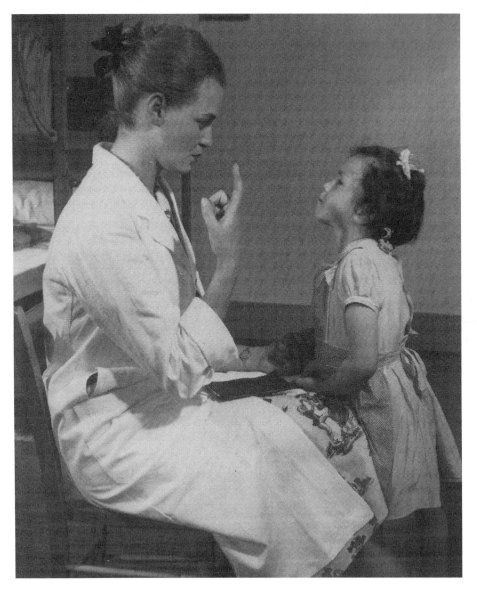

Miss Tanner, giving Maureen a Speech Therapy lesson.
Photographer: Morland Braithwaite.

Some of the parents and the children also met in Mrs Mailer's house in Wychall Lane – I have a photograph of us. Her daughter, Janet, was also disabled. We were friends together and you'd see how other people were dealing with their own disability... and get ideas from that. So there we were, meeting up occasionally and preparing the new school in Harborne. I've got all of this, about the school, on CD. It's a film called *Steps to Independence* – made by Mr Filkin – whose son produced *Tomorrow's World*. My co-writer, Shirley, and I have watched some of these films together. There are several other films, made by Mr Morland Braithwaite, the photographer, who used to have a shop in Moseley.

As soon as we arrived at the new school, we were taken off our feet. The physiotherapist, Miss Hyatt, looked at us and sent us off to the various departments. Those with speech difficulties went off to the Speech Therapist, a Miss Rosser, to be assessed.

Mr Howell, who adapted the school chairs to our individual needs, had an antique shop in Selly Oak. If you were allowed to, you could walk, but I'm not quite sure what they decided about me, although at this stage, relaxation became the name of the game – terribly boring!

It meant that in the afternoon you had an hour's relaxation on a bed: I managed to get out of that most of the time!

The babies of the class used to lie on beds, I was just that bit older. But when I got home at night, I had to lie on the floor for half an hour and listen to the wireless as it was known in those days, rather than the radio. I'd listen to *Music While You Work*, from a quarter to seven; there were several programmes that I listened to. The wireless had a great influence on me, because I could use my imagination. It was absolute agony, lying on the floor. *Dick Barton, Special Agent*, fired my imagination, then they took it off, in 1952, for something called the bloomin' *Archers*!

Some of the actors in that, actually lived very close to where I live now: Harry Oakes, who played Dan Archer and Wimbledon Tennis Champion, Ann Haydon Jones all lived in Yarningdale Road, Kings Heath. Ann began as a table tennis player, then progressed to tennis.

So we were taken down to Physio, assessed and then Morland Braithwaite took pictures of us, doing various things. What we didn't realise at the time is that they were experimenting with us – learning about the spastic condition.

As far as I was concerned, they decided that a spasm had pulled out my left hip. Spastics can have a spasm any time. So I walked with a limp. It was decided that I should wear calipers with a join at the knee. Now once you've taken on these leg aids you can never do without them.

At times I was going to hospital for my eyes – *and* for my legs; they even suggested at one time that I might have tuberculosis. So they wanted me to go to a Tuberculosis Clinic in Great Charles Street, Birmingham City Centre, but my mother declined that: she felt I was going to hospital enough times already.

'From little acorns do mighty oak trees grow'. David in Class 2, 2nd Floor, Carlson House School. This particular classroom later became the Staffroom.

We had two porters working around the school, doing odd jobs. Mrs Brown lived from 1922 to 2014... and we continued to keep in touch. I used to imagine that Mr Brown had a wooden leg, because he had a limp – and that he screwed this leg on, every morning!

Meanwhile, I was in and out of hospital. They decided when I was nine that I should have my eyes straightened, at the Children's Hospital. I was knock-kneed, goofy and I squinted, so they covered my good eye up, to make my lazy eye work better. But I said,

"I can't see." They said, "Don't be so silly!"

They took me to films but I couldn't look at them. That went on for about six weeks. When I was nine, they took the patch off and realised that I couldn't see out of the eye. I said,

"I've been telling you that for years." That is the eye that had haemorrhaged, when I was being born! I've only got one eye that I can see out of, so I'm obviously very keen on that.

They tried several things to get my hip back in, but it wouldn't go, so they hung me upside-down, from the ceiling! On a frame – at another hospital.

It was going to be a longer stay, 'til I went off to Saint Gerard's, next to Father Hudson's Homes, at Coleshill. They didn't want to know what was wrong with you; they were more interested in what your religion was! It was Roman Catholic, so I had to buy a rosary, for 2/6d – (about 12½p nowadays!)

I was hung up on this frame and I caught dysentery, from the rats under the floorboards... so don't talk to me about Health and Safety! This was at the height of the Polio Epidemic; most of the people in there had had polio. They were being kept there from the age of 5, until they were better, with no education: the nuns got a Grant for the number of bodies in the place.

You didn't get anything to eat unless your parents brought it in, although there was an old lady there called 'Ye-Ye', who would cook something:

"What's for tea tonight Ye-Ye?" "Oh, 'Bread-and-Scrape'. Here – have these baked beans!"

My mother and father used to come at the weekends and bring some Exeter Stew that could be heated up, until my mother tripped up and threw it over one of the nuns!

Anyway, they eventually decided that this was not going to work, so I remember the happy day, when the nurses just whipped the Elastoplast off my leg. When I screamed they told me not to be such a baby – and there was the blood and everything – hanging down on this Elastoplast!

I was in that hospital for two or three months. Unfortunately, I missed Roy Rogers and Trigger coming to the school, but I managed to get his autograph by other means.

My parents forcibly removed me from that hospital and I went back to school. But by that time I was a nervous wreck! I was thin and wouldn't eat; because I was losing weight I had to go and see the school doctor, Doctor Mole, every month.

So I came back home and was walking around – but with this limp. Once I had moved to Carlson House, I changed from Mr Hughes, to a Mr Innes, who was an Orthopaedic Surgeon. He came to the school every week, on a Thursday morning. He looked at your records and what progress you were making. He was very tall; dressed in a pin-striped suit. We used to call him 'Mr Beanpole'! I dreaded seeing him, because he always hurt me.

By this time both of my legs were straight. I did a bit of walking, but mostly moved around on my bottom, using my arms.

Eventually they decided that I could benefit, possibly, from having my left hip fixed. There was a gentleman in Manchester, Mr Charnley, who was experimenting with hips, so it was decided that I would go there. But I got very upset, at one stage, because decisions were being made about me, without consulting me, so I was then included in this consultation. You had to be a certain age before that could happen, when your bones became more solid.

So in 1954 I went up to Manchester to see Mr Charnley at the Park Hospital. He was pioneering a new operation to fix hip joints, so when he offered to operate on me, I agreed. It involved breaking my leg, pushing it out there; pinning it and then bending it back down. That would mean that I would be four inches shorter on one leg.

My parents left me at the hospital. I was amongst all of the old men, who were dying – and what-have-you! There was an eighty-five-year-old who was all strung up, because he'd broken his leg. This other patient behind me, I don't know what was the matter with him, but he swore blind that this other bloke would only go out of there in his box!

So I sat there, listening to all of this. They were all having visitors – I was having none.

Then one day the gentleman with a broken leg started saying,

"I must get up in the morning and I must plant my potatoes!" So they moved him to a single room. Eventually he died, and the other guy was ecstatic!

"I told you he was going to die!" And there I am... stranded.

Two beds up was a man with gangrene: every time they touched him he screamed the place down! They had to keep rolling him.

All of this sounds totally nightmarish – but I thought it was funny! Whilst I was in there, a gentleman came in, dressed in women's clothing. He'd had his leg off, but it had sent him a bit 'doolally'! They put him in a single room, but when they went to fetch him he'd gone. They were looking under the bed – everywhere! But he'd opened the window, gone down the drainpipe with one leg and was in the shrubbery, carving himself a crutch!

So when they got him back in, all night he was saying,

"I won't do it again Sister! I won't do it again" ... and I'm listening to all of this.

Anyway, they encased me in plaster, with my leg pinned – and sent me home to Birmingham. The Manchester ambulance had brought me down and the Birmingham ambulance took me back up. So when they lifted me out of the plaster cast, after six weeks, they caught this leg, it went crack and I went into spasm! Completely... absolutely... couldn't speak; couldn't do anything.

They bunged me in the ambulance and drove me eighty-four miles, a quivering wreck, back to Birmingham and into my bed at home... on the ground floor. I really thought I'd had it.

Eventually I calmed down and was able to stand up. I was using two elbow crutches and walking about. I read this book about Douglas Bader, by Paul Brickhill, called *Reach for the Sky*. Readers may recall that Kenneth More played the leading role in the subsequent film.

When I read the book I thought: 'if he can bloomin' well do it, then so can I.' I got my elbow crutches and decided that, however difficult it was going to be, I was going to walk! So I walked everywhere, for a day, then my right leg went in a spasm and went bent.

I was supposed to be taking O' Levels in quite a few subjects, but they went by the wayside, as these further problems developed. I was still registered at Carlson House, but I went back up to the Park Hospital to finish what Mr Charnley had done; I was an example of being able to walk about.

Then when my leg started to bend they couldn't understand why it was hurting me so much, telling me not to be a 'titty-baby' and so forth. They'd got this girl sitting with me, while I was lying down and doing exercises. I was in absolute tears in front of her. They were leaping up and down on my leg, saying,

"That doesn't hurt, does it?!" When I told them that it did, they put a splint back on my leg and they'd straighten it every day. This was around 1958.

I was in Class 2 at Carlson House, but then they started a Study Group, when we were due to do O' Levels. There were two people in it: Anthony Sutton and John Lynes (now both deceased)… and I joined them.

Now I can be incredibly stupid at times, when I'm agitated. I was what they call a 'Late Developer'. Before I went into hospital, in about 1952, a Mr Collins inspired me and I really started to take an interest. For my O' Levels I got English Literature, English Language and History through the Oxford and Cambridge Board: you were allowed extra time.

But the Northern Matriculation Board wouldn't allow us extra time. When I was doing my Maths and Arithmetic I knew the answers, but I couldn't get it down quickly enough. So I took the London Chamber of Commerce Maths exam at school too. As I was sitting up, I was able to write, although it was always in the hay fever season!

Due to my medical situation, I took the History O' Level twice: the first time it covered 1066 – 1485; the second time it was 1688 – 1815… but that was a different teacher. I graduated into a Study Group, which then meant that Anthony and I were taught by an Irish gent, Mr Docherty, who had polio… but he was a hopeless teacher! He just read the chapter in front of what he was teaching you, then he went off for three days and you worked on your own – that was the way it worked.

You're supposed to give your pupils some insight into events, to aid their interpretation of what actually happened. Well he made a few points: we had a little discussion.

I passed my History exam, but I failed my French. I was too nervous. I could do the written exam but I failed the Oral part of it. So I got 39%. I went to Belgium later. The first thing you say is, "Comment allez-vous?" The reply is "Ca va bien merci." And then I'm bloomin' lost! I couldn't speak it at all.

Anthony, to whom my book is dedicated, came from Dudley. He gave the impression that he'd got a reasonable amount of money; because he was not in the Birmingham conurbation his parents had to pay for his transport to school.

He got Mr Docherty to teach him at home. So he passed his 'A Level'. Although he had a speech defect, he did Spanish and Russian. He was one of the first (if not *the* first) disabled student at Birmingham University.

When Anthony went to University that left me and John Lynes. John was the sort of person who had to study twenty-four hours a day. He passed his exams and went to work at Cadburys, in the Export Department. So that left me on my own. I've spent a very lonely life really.

Anthony Toye was at Carlson House. His parents were 'born-again-Christians'. They didn't like him being called Tony: his name was Anthony! They thought that he was disabled because of their sins in a previous life. His arm and leg on one side of his body were disabled.

If they felt that they had progressed with you as far as they could, you moved on to a normal school. He went to somewhere in Halesowen so I lost touch with him.

When I was on my own, they decided that some young girls from down below could come up occasionally and have classes with me. This is when I met Mrs Purcell, who I liked. She lived in Dorridge … and was a good History Teacher. Her husband was Head of Religious Knowledge, on BBC Radio.

The Welfare Department helped too. I was fortunate that I went to the *Helping Hand Youth Club*, which was a stepping stone between school and the outside world. I lived for Friday night when I met up with my friends, who I went about with. I went there until I was 21. I was on the radio programme that they ran from there, reading out the 'Promise' which was about our Youth Club.

Paul Cadbury said that even in the most stringent days of financial cutbacks, there was always money available for any project, if you knew where to look, as long as you have the right connections – and of course he had. His Trust helped the *MSA* to keep afloat, on several occasions, by what they called Interest Free Loans. He also donated all of the films of pupils that were taken for medical purposes: they were supposed to have gone to somewhere in the Royal Orthopaedic Hospital, bearing in mind that, as well as Uffculme, Moseley Hall was a Cadbury House.

According to Pete Millington, who we'll be meeting in more detail in a later chapter:

"My friend, Paul Boaler, has a severe speech impediment; he encounters all manner of prejudice; he'll be speaking to people, but they'll answer him as if he's a child. Paul went to school with Maureen, David's future wife, at Carlson House. I'm still in touch with Paul – he lives in Harborne. David knows him too."

You didn't have friends from the school, as such, because they were scattered throughout Birmingham, and I was unlikely to see them in the evenings.

Now when you're meeting able-bodied people who are kind to you, in an atmosphere where most people look upon you with a little bit of apprehension,

Top left: Stephen Quayle. Top right: Paul Cadbury.
Bottom left: Earl Carlson's parents. Bottom right: Earl Carlson.
BY KIND PERMISSION OF CEREBRAL PALSY MIDLANDS.

then you tend to warm to them; they become attached to you, but when they disappear you are heartbroken, because your number of friends disappears.

In my youth I had two friends that I can remember. There was Roy, an able-bodied boy, who lived at the bottom of Pakefield Road. We were quite big friends and then eventually we broke apart. Then there was somebody else called Michael, who lived in the Avenue. He was very kind and we played games, then he moved on and I was left stranded. My aunt told me, thirty years later, that they only came to play with me because I had more toys than they had! I was quite upset by the loss of these relationships. I'm happier with disabled friends, as a result.

When I was at school, I belonged to a Scout Troop. We went to a place called Woodlarks, at Farnham, in Surrey, where we camped for a week at a time, sleeping on the ground, because there were groundsheets and a sleeping bag. I was 11 or 12 years of age, at that time. We took part in activities in the forest and had camp fires at night. There was an area where, if you were a little bit shy, you could go undercover and be under canvas. That's what I did. This was the first time I'd left home – and my Mummy and Daddy! So that was quite a shock.

In the Scouts we also went to Gilwell: the disabled equivalent of a Jubilee – which was called *Agoon*. We represented our country there and met some foreign scouts. Gilwell was the Headquarters of the Scout Movement. We also met Lady Baden Powell, who was much younger than her husband, although she was getting on a bit by then.

We went abroad, in 1958, to an *Expo Exhibition* in Belgium, where the *Atomium* was built and we visited a lot of the pavilions. There were a number of pavilions that we couldn't get into because they had steps. Cinerama was the great moment at the time. Mr John Fennell was the Scoutmaster, who lived in Victoria Road, opposite the school. He took somebody with him, to help us.

I was in quite a lot of pain, because of my right leg bending – trying to straighten it and all the rest of it – there's a picture of me, looking in absolute agony! I went with the Scouts... the Handicapped Branch. It was the Belgian *World's Fair*.

The gentlemen wanted to go to the toilet, so they went into the Hungarian Pavilion, but soon shot out of the toilet, because there were ladies on their hands and knees, sweeping the urine away, as the gentlemen did it!

If we stood on the dustbin, we could see the *Atomium*, from where we stayed. It was a restaurant that was in the balls of an atom, that went round and round. You could have a meal up there, if you could afford it. It's still there today. So that was the first time that I went away.

In 1974 when Carlson House ran into financial difficulties, the Paul S. Cadbury Trust loaned the Midland Spastic Society £20,000, interest free, to keep the school going. At the same time he persuaded the local authorities to increase their contributions. He also funded a series of cerebral palsy studies at Aston and Birmingham Universities.

Mary Fletcher was also a pupil at the school:

"I knew David as an older boy – I was down in the first class at Carlson House. I'm four years younger than him.

"I was around eighteen months old, perhaps a bit younger; when children start to sit up. I wasn't doing that – so I wasn't walking. I had a twin brother who was doing all of these things. Eventually Mum and Dad discovered that I had cerebral palsy, which was then called 'spastic'. In the fullness of time they managed to get me into Carlson House.

"I also had an older brother – John. Together with my Mum and Dad they all encouraged me to do things that sometimes the school didn't agree with. My Dad worked in engineering; before Mum was married she was a shop assistant. But as there were three of us, so she no longer worked.

"My parents took a very positive approach and treated me, as far as possible, like an able-bodied person. My twin brother, David, attended mainstream school. He went to the primary school, which was just up the road from us, and had an education, which I felt was much better than the one that I had.

"But at the time this was happening, I was just focusing on what I was doing; it was only with hindsight that I reached that conclusion about what was happening.

"Without my family, I wouldn't be the person that I am today and have the confidence to do the things that I do. I was more able-bodied than Dave Barnsley and could walk with sticks; earlier still, when I was at school, I could walk without them! The problem was that I couldn't stop! Which could be very awkward. I always had a pair of sticks, but only used them when I really needed to.

"In a later chapter, David will be telling you about his second wife, Maureen Pritchard. I knew her from when we were in the same class at school. We became friends. It wasn't only Maureen: there was Ann and Sandra – we used to go round in a foursome.

"We had loads of fun and Maureen would come and stay at our house. She used to love that, because she quite liked my brothers! We had great fun at school – she was really nice.

"David said he found out more recently, that even when she was young, Maureen had suicidal tendencies. She didn't ever talk about it, but it was there. She was so frustrated because she was quite severely disabled, although she overcame it very well.

"Because I grew up with her and we were at school together, we became quite close. But then when we left school we didn't see each other for quite a while. So when we met up again, it was quite difficult to tune in to her," Mary concludes.

The school was eventually closed by Birmingham City Council, in 1982 for various reasons. Looking back I enjoyed it and overall it was a pleasant time, but it was a different era. I was at Carlson School from the age of seven until eighteen, when I left school and got a job, so that was eleven years.

My life has been good and I put the basis of all of that down to my childhood years, in Carlson House School.

Chapter Three

Work, Rest and Play

In February 1959 Buddy Holly, one of my favourite singers, died in a plane crash, near Clear Lake Minnesota. He was travelling to his next show in Moorhead, Minnesota. Also killed in the crash were Ritchie Valens, The Big Bopper, and the pilot, Roger Peterson. Later, Don McLean immortalized the tragedy in his song, 'The Day the Music Died'.

'The Sound of Music' was performed for the very first time, at the Lunt-Fontanne Theatre, New York, on 16 November (music by Richard Rodgers, lyrics by Oscar Hammerstein). Cliff Richard's 'Livin' Doll' and 'Travellin' Light' entered our Hit Parade.

Also in 1959, The British Post Office introduced post codes in July – and the new Mini Minor first appeared on our roads.

David Barnsley

That same year, having spent 11 years of my childhood at Carlson House School in Harborne, I left school aged 18, to work for *Lucas's*.

The school staff had been going round local businesses looking for employment opportunities for school leavers from Carlson House; *Lucas's* was one of the employers whom they approached.

Mrs Marlow, the school's second headmistress, told this company that they had a prospective school leaver with O' Levels. I was sent for an interview and given the job.

Mrs Marlow's 'Headmistress Report', regarding my progress at Carlson House, read as follows:

David has always worked conscientiously well throughout his stay at Carlson House. He has been thoughtful of others and reliable. I shall follow his future with interest and trust that he will keep in touch.

It has been advised that he follow a course of training, when he leaves in July, in commercial subjects, before seeking employment. Now that he has been provided with a motorised chair, getting to and from a place of work will not be a problem to him.

She continued with a summary of my examination results and then concluded:

David has our sincere good wishes for his future success!

So I left school in July 1959 and started work at *Lucas Electrical*, Great King Street, on 7 September 1959.

I was scared stiff before the interview, but they were quite pleasant. They said I could have a job in 'Supplier's Accounts'. Unfortunately, I was rather slow. You had to match all the goods inwards with the invoices, in alphabetical order and staple them together.

Passport photo of David, taken shortly after he began working at Lucas Electrical.

A bloke came round with a book to check how many you'd done. It never occurred to me to lie like everyone else – they never counted them anyway. So I was deemed to be too slow and given all the dirty little jobs to do in the office instead. I stuck at it though, because five pounds seventeen and sixpence was a lot of money in those days. From that my father took £3 for accommodation; the petrol and oil for my Trike was 5/4d a gallon. So even though they gave me all the dead filing to do, at least I had a job.

After only a few months in this first job, I was to experience the dreaded cold shoulder of discrimination, familiar to many disabled people of my generation. When others were moved to a new floor, which could only be accessed by stairs, I was left virtually on my own. I stayed on M3 whilst everyone else moved to G7. We were on the clock and I used to come up in an old lift, to sit on my own. The supervisor would come in just to see if I was in, then leave again. After six months I was pretty cheesed off with this arrangement, but eventually they all came back down and I was glad of the company again.

They had a merit rating, to see if you were satisfactory at your job. The supervisor told me,

"You're close to getting the push: you don't know the section and you talk too much, so I'm going to have you sitting next to me, where I can keep my eye on you." Well of course, I didn't know the section, because it was up on another floor!

During my early years at *Lucas's*, I got fed up, seeing my colleagues being given promotion whilst I remained on a low grade. You'd see the supervisor taking people to one side and he'd tell them they'd got a rise, saying, "But don't tell anyone," and they'd all go into the gents and find they'd got a rise of 5 shillings 25 pence. They put me on checking invoices against the orders for a while, which no one else ever did – before or after me. It should have been Grade 8 money, but I was still paid Grade 5.

For the next few years people would come in and ask me how to do things and I'd tell them, because I'd been there for a long time, but then they'd get good, high-powered jobs and I'd remain stuck on Grade 5.

One day when we arrived for work, a stonking great hole had suddenly appeared, about 12-foot down, in the road. Luckily the security bloke in the box had not been dropped down the hole!

Bear in mind that the factory had a vault built into the wall... from the *Lord Byron*, a little bit further down the road was the *Duke of Cambridge* Public House! That's been flattened: there's just a blue plaque there now: 'Lucas's was here!'

A friend of mine, Bill Fraser, eventually convinced me that the company were taking me for a ride, so I demanded an interview with Personnel. After making my own enquiries about accessible parts of the company, I pushed myself forward for a move to Great Hampton Street and was finally put on Grade 8 money.

Joseph Lucas Electrical Limited, Great King Street, David's place of employment from 1959 – 1976.

A manager there told me that because I'd been so patient they would give me the Grade 8, an increase of £2 after 5 years with the company – actually the minimum for the grade. I recall he was so pleased with himself that he came down three times that day, to tell me I'd got the £2 rise!

I was dealing with the accounts T-Z… we'd come in on a Saturday morning, to make those payments. One of the big accounts was *Trico Falbert*: they manufactured windscreen wipers. So I'd have a cheque for £50,000 on my desk. But I wouldn't be able to release it until they'd got the money in from the customer's account.

The man would ring up and ask me if I'd got his cheque for him, so you have to start lying:

"It's out for the directors."

"Can I speak to the directors please?!"

"Sorry – they're in a meeting."

"Can I speak to his secretary?"

"She's with him – ring back this afternoon!"

So that's how it went on.

We also had temporary staff that the company paid agencies for – which was more than we were getting paid; some of the agency staff were there for longer than the permanent staff. But all this time I was also learning about life.

I eventually got into operating accounts; on the same floor but in a different department. That was a more satisfactory job. I was on the Overheads, so I had to phone around the factory to get the overhead figures, on a monthly basis. It was a bit awkward because some people rattled the figures off. So I bought myself an 18-inch ruler, for 12 shillings and sixpence. I used that along the line.

In 1972 there was a Miner's Strike. When the lights went out, we were on a massive floor – in total darkness! All we could do was sit there – and I was always terrified of having to go up and down in the lift... because during the strike the lift wouldn't work! They started telling us when the lights would be going out. So instead of working 8.30 – 5.30, we started at 12 and worked until 10 o'clock at night! Then drove home in the pitch dark of the street.

In spite of these difficulties, I was a loyal employee of *Lucas's*, staying with them for 28 years. Eventually I became a supervisor, working at Great King Street until 1976, before moving to *Lucas Aerospace* in Shirley. I left in 1988.

I didn't actually have much authority because the person who had given me the job left – my wife also left too. So I was a nervous wreck there for the first 4 years and the person sitting next to me didn't want to tell me too much.

In contrast to my situation, my friend, the late Joe McGuire, was able-bodied until the age of 23. Then suddenly, 'out-of-the-blue', he had an awful shock!

"At that time I was working on a *Bryant's* site in Town," Joe recalls. "I went to work as usual in the morning, but I began to feel more and more unwell. I had a chat with the Foreman, telling him that I had to go home. I went home on the bus. After I got off the bus I had a small distance to travel, but as I made it to the house my legs were giving out.

"The doctor had been treating me for a pulled muscle – in other words – he didn't know exactly what was wrong! He was called, but by the time he arrived, I was paralysed from the waist down! It started from my toes and felt as if the numbness was gradually working its way over me, like waves. I was lying on the bed, and as I waited for the doctor, the symptoms were as if I was at the seashore: the waves were lapping over my feet and coming up over my body.

"As that sensation got further and further I lost the feeling in that part below my chest – and also movement, within just a few hours.

"By the time the doctor arrived this had already happened. He was going to have me admitted to Selly Oak Hospital, but they had no department to deal with such matters as the spinal cord, so I was sent to the Queen Elizabeth.

"I had an operation at the QE but because it was so close to the spinal cord they could not remove all of the tumour. Had they done so, the outcome would have been worse than if they left it.

"I was there for about a month. They told my relatives, including my sister, because they could do nothing further for me at the QE, that I had about four months to a year to live.

"I was 'bed-blocking', so they sent me back to Selly Oak, into a Geriatric Ward. My sister's name is Mary – she's older than me. I cannot say that I adapted well when I was there in Selly Oak. Because as I said – Geriatric Ward: all of the old chaps were aged from seventy to eighty; quite a few of them were dying off," recalls Joe.

I admire Joe for the fact that he had to adjust to becoming disabled. I've been like that all my life – and it never bothered me until I went to work. Then, from that period on, it became a problem.

But I cannot understand how a man, at twenty-three years old, can lie in a Geriatric Ward, with no possible future – and no hope of surviving beyond a few months. Nobody dreamt that he would live to be 79 – this year!

"I couldn't do anything to help myself," Joe continues. "I had to be lifted out of bed, toileted et cetera. Although they did their best, the nurses and other staff had no idea about how to treat somebody who was paralysed."

Shirley and I watched the Documentary, about the radical changes that Doctor Ludwig Guttmann (later Sir Ludwig) made in treatment, at Stoke Mandeville Hospital, from the mid-1940s. It's called *The Best of Men*. It explores the pioneering work of this German Doctor, from 1899 – 1980.

In September 1943 the British Government asked Guttmann to establish the *National Spinal Injuries Unit* at Stoke Mandeville Hospital, for injured servicemen. His revolutionary new treatment was to play a vital part in their recovery. Further information about him may be found in an Appendix, at the back of our book.

Before the doctor's arrival the staff didn't have a clue about how best to treat the wounded soldiers in their care. They had them all plastered up and just lying in bed, with no exercise or mental stimulation, and he just totally turned that situation around. So in 1944, he was well ahead of his time.

But what Joe's experience seems to show is that even in the 1960s, the situation hadn't improved, to any significant extent, at certain hospitals.

"Yes – and remember that when somebody becomes paralysed and is lying down for some time, their body hasn't got used to it. They're not supposed to be sat up immediately. But the nursing staff knew nothing about that," Joe continues.

"I was in bed for two or three weeks after I came back to Selly Oak – lying down all the time. Then they decided that they would have to get me out and sitting up. But of course when they sat me up I just passed out – because the blood wasn't getting to my brain! Having no strength in my back I couldn't sit up – so I was hanging over my chair for grim death – they hadn't got the sense to put a cushion on the chair!

"They took me to Physiotherapy and I was left sitting there all afternoon, while a few of them looked at me, from a distance, then I was taken back to the ward. That was the sum total of my physiotherapy!

"I did have Radiotherapy, but they were still thinking about me passing on.

"Social Services told me about *The Beeches*, in 1962; a year later, in 1963, I'd moved in there.

"The lady that came to see me, when I transferred back from the QE to Selly Oak, to avoid bed-blocking, told me that *The Beeches* was in the process of being built. I didn't hear anything else until a year later, when she came back and told me I'd been granted permission.

"They arranged for one of the special vehicles to pick me up and take me there. *The Beeches* was opened by the Queen in May 1960 and people were just in the process of moving in.

"Younger disablement was anything up to sixty-five and there were all sorts of disabilities. There were people in wheelchairs; people who could walk a bit; people with Parkinson's; MS – all sorts of conditions," Joe recalls.

"The woman in charge was a nurse, but the staff were just ordinary people: just people who needed a job. They did their best, but it was a difficult situation. Although the homes were supposed to have been built for disabled people, the toilets were not at all suitable. The staff had to do all the lifting.

"As David will know, toilet facilities at many of the places the disabled have visited over the years were often a problem, in terms of being able to actually get past the doors.

"But I reckon that you've always been quite adventurous David – compared to myself," Joe concludes.

Pete Millington's *Disability Timeline* has its own special section, in Chapter 8 of this book. Here he describes the Pre-1950 situation:

"The West and Europe's view on disability often changes after wars, especially the First and Second World Wars. There were vast numbers of people who served their country, coming back with profound levels of impairment (the gas in the trenches and so on)," Pete explains.

"The country was supposed to provide 'A Land Fit for Heroes', although often that expectation was never met. But it *did* foster a different approach to disability. All disabled people benefitted from that change.

"After the Second World War, in the 1950s, it was a very aspirational society that we were living in," Pete continues. "The National Health Service was founded and there was a lot of liberal advances, such as the Employment Act, which said that after 1948 employers had to employ a certain percentage of disabled people.

"So pre-1950s it was more institution based, but post 1950 it was more Carer based. The Victorians founded a lot of the Institutions, whether they were asylums or 'colonies' as they used to call them. So a disabled child would be taken away from his parents and grow up in an Institution.

"The 1950s, being more Carer led, allowed parents to take an active role for the very first time, by refusing to follow the former approach; either by making sure that their disabled child went to a more humane institution or by trying to care for him at home... and taking him to a more progressive school like Carlson House. The *Spastic Society* was also founded around that time," Pete concludes.

Chapter Four

A Trike on the Queensway (and other Motoring Tales)

Generally-speaking, people were usually helpful, but what I don't like is people feeling sorry for me. You make life according to what you want to do. I say to my children: 'You can always listen to advice; if you think it's good – fair enough. If you don't – don't bother!'

Roger Robinson

The first holiday that we went on was in 1962. Roger Robinson will tell you all about that. There was a newspaper article about it.

One Saturday night, three or four of us went on a trip. I stopped to turn the map over, in Edmonton, just off the North Circular Road, but the trike wouldn't go again. We had two sets of points: one for going forward; then you turned it off, spun the engine in a different way to go backwards: another set of points.

We stopped at three o'clock in the afternoon and we were there until nine o'clock at night! The *RAC* did come out and reluctantly looked at my vehicle, because although there were specialist repairers, they were closed on a weekend. I always broke down on a Saturday night!

They eventually managed to get the points set; it was difficult – you had to move the wheel axle, and all sorts of things. And drop the suspension down so that they could get to the points.

Managed to get it going. We started off, in the dark, going down the road to our destination... about seventeen-and-three-quarter miles! Then seventeen miles; sixteen and three-quarter; sixteen-and-a-half and so forth – all the way to Southend! Almost to Leigh-on-Sea, where we turned off, to go to the seafront in Southend.

The *Arundel Hotel* was run by the *Spastic Society*. We arrived late at night, then spent the weekend waiting for the local repairers, which was in Essex.

The Road to Independence: David's very first Trike, with a 197cc 2-stroke, detuned, Go-Kart engine – (a 'Puddle Jumper!'). Photographed on Roy Cox's drive, 71 Wassall Road, Halesowen.

I didn't get much enjoyment from the holiday, because I was worried to death. But we were there for a week. We went down the longest pier – in Southend – (Sarfend!) – which was a mile-and-a-quarter. It was serviced by former Underground trains, made by *ACEDES (AC)* who also provided the labour to build the trikes... and for racing cars at Le Mans.

So we went up and down the pier. At that time there was a boat that went over to France, called the *Medway Queen*. Tell our readers more about the holidays to 'Sarfend' Roger – we had some really funny moments!

Roger elaborates: "It was a long way to go in a Trike, because they only had small engines. David broke down, just the other side of London; we had to wait for the *RAC* to arrive to get David's car mobile. The *RAC* man asked David how much further he had to go. We said Southend, so he said, 'Whatever you do, don't stop the car!'

"To the annoyance of the hotel owners, we arrived at midnight, on the Sunday. But we had a really good time there.

"We arranged to go to a wrestling event; we went for a meal on the Friday evening and were due to return on the Saturday," Roger continues. "We went along the pier every morning. I tried to baffle this fella, because I spoke in a different accent every morning. In the end he said to me, 'Where are you actually from?' I could have said, 'My mother and father,' but I *did* say Birmingham!

"I think the guy was a local; he worked on the pier, was middle-aged – and always seemed to be in the same spot… sitting at the entrance to the pier. It was really good," remembers Roger.

There was actually a wrestler who carried a handbag – Romeo Joe Critchley! It was all a bit of a show – which reminds Shirley of a time when Pat Roach's mother, Dolly, hit the referee with her handbag, because she thought he was being unfair to Pat, with his scoring!

But anyway, the manageress of the *Arundel* used to show films of local events and fundraising. Bob Monkhouse had a big input into that, at the time, because his son, Gary, was severely handicapped so she showed films of that – if you remember, Roger.

Then one night, we'd just bought the first Beatles LP record and were playing it on a record player, messing about and being fairly raucous. The manageress asked if we'd like to see some still photographs of ladies with no clothes on – so that was the height of our erotic experience – in the early years of the 'Swinging Sixties'!

Although I was embarrassed, she went up considerably in our estimation. She hailed from South Africa, but I can't remember her name. She eventually got married and moved on.

We went on several holidays to Southend, but on one of the holidays Roger cricked his neck, so he was in absolute agony!

We met one or two people from other areas. We enjoyed going to the *Kurzel* to watch the wrestling. It had an aluminium roof. Ladies get very excited, watching the wrestling!

Roger's provided us with a copy of that same *Birmingham Post & Mail* article, entitled *Holiday for Three by Invalid Car*. It's written by a 'Mail Staff Reporter' (name and date not available), although judging by our ages the article must have been written in 1961:

> *Three never-say-die young Birmingham men, all physically handicapped, went on holiday today – and only one of them can walk. They left a house in Yardley Wood in their invalid cars for a week's holiday, at a specially equipped hotel at Westcliffe-on-Sea, near Southend.*
>
> *Seventeen-year-old electrical assembler Roger Robinson, of 162 School Road Yardley Wood, is the only one who can walk. His two friends, twenty-year-old Mr David Barnsley, a clerk of Kings Norton and Birmingham University student, twenty-three-year-old Mr Anthony Sutton of Dudley, go around in invalid chairs.*
>
> *They met at the 'MSA Centre for the Handicapped'. The 134-mile trip to Southend is the longest journey that they've undertaken.*

When Roger was born, doctors told his mother, Mrs Faye Robinson, 'Your son will never walk.' But on his seventh birthday he did walk, for the first time in his life – a few halting steps across the ward at the Woodlands Hospital, Northfield.

Six operations since then have strengthened his legs. Roger said, 'I can walk quite well now. David and Anthony cannot, so I will be able to help them to get in and out of their cars.'

As the three blue cars moved off, Mrs Robinson said, 'All three have such wonderful courage. They are always looking for things to do and help themselves to lead lives as normal as possible.'

Roger explains: "My Mum arranged the interview – I didn't know anything about it! I first met David at the Carlson House Club on a Friday. We seemed to get on very well. I was 15 or 16 years old when I met him. David was two years older than me. The club was called the *Helping Hand Youth Club*.

"It was a relatively new building, next door to the school; we met there each Friday. David came over to introduce himself – I think he was the Chairman. He said, 'I'm David and this is what we do, each week.' They played games and all sorts of things: Draughts and Chess – but I'm not very good at that! There was Table Tennis, but only for those who were able to play it.

"We all used to end up having a chat: David introduced me to Anthony Sutton – and from there we had a really good time.

"We talked about work, because David was an office clerk and I was an electrical assembler – being posh! We'd go to the cinema sometimes; a couple of times we went to *Silverstone* – that was very good – in the days of Stirling Moss. Stirling used to do several motor races at each meeting – the *Grand Prix* – but he also drove in all the other car races.

"*Barnes Close* was a *YMCA* place. We went there once or twice a year, from a Friday to Sunday evening. On those occasions we had games, a Treasure Hunt – and just a general chit-chat.

"We also had Car Trials in the trikes and then the fastest car," Roger remembers. "David told me that he was always competitive – he liked to win... even though he didn't always. I just wanted to take part... that was the best thing. If I came first I came first...no worries!

"David has always been smartly dressed and well presented – and you could go to him for advice. I'd ask him about the best way to go about things. I didn't have the knowledge that he had about solving problems, so it was very helpful for me to be able to take that on board. David's quite broadly educated... and we both have a sense of humour!

"When my Mum saw me walk for the first time at Woodlands Hospital, it was between parallel bars," he continues. "My twin sister, Annette, was as normal as can be; that's how we found about my spasticity/cerebral palsy, because I wasn't sitting up – and was flopping all over the place!

"So my Mum took me to the GP first and then to the hospital, where she was told that I'd never be able to walk. Usually, with twins, it's the girl who's disabled, not the boy. So my case was more unusual.

"I can remember going to hospital at one particular time, just for a check-up. I was lying on a stretcher with my eyes closed. My Mum was talking to another person, telling them that I'd never be able walk. When I heard her say that I thought: 'We'll see!'

"It was a real challenge for me. I didn't go to school until I came out of hospital, when I was 7," Roger explains. "Mum had a terrible job to get me into a school. She wanted me to go to a normal school, but they wouldn't accept me."

In another section of our book, we examine that question, in more detail: under what circumstances should a disabled child be educated in a mainstream school?

"My father passed away when I was eleven months old," Roger recalls. "Like David, I was interested in motor racing – that's why I went with him to *Silverstone*. We'd go there once a year, for the *British Grand Prix*, which was completely different from today's event, because the crowds were much smaller and they didn't have the sophisticated technology that they have now. The event was sponsored by *Central TV*.

"We also enjoyed going to cinemas: the Odeon, New Street; the Scala. We went to see the *Indianapolis 500*, the year that Jim Clarke won it."

According to my biographer, Shirley, Martin Hone organized the *Birmingham Super Prix*. She got to know him and his wife, Patti, quite well, while working on Eddie Fewtrell's Biography, *King of Clubs*. Martin also owned the Opposite Lock nightclub.

"Returning to the subject of the *Three Musketeers*, David, Anthony and myself were good pals with each other," explains Roger. "My memories of David and Anthony are that they were both well educated. Anthony used to do translation work too. Sadly, he passed away in 2012. So, we'd go on holiday; to the cinema; competitive rallies; other events involving Trikes.

"Like David, there were some hair-raising moments with my Trike," remembers Roger. "I used to visit a friend of mine, who lived in Northfield. One Saturday when I was coming back in the Trike, I was coming up Parson's Hill. I nearly got to the top, pulled the clutch in, to change gear – and the clutch cable snapped! I had to roll back down the hill, to the nearest phone box!

"When I was just 17 and I had my Trike to get about, my Mum saw a job advertised in the *Evening Mail*: 'Bench-hands required for assembly work'.

"On the Monday I went up to Stockfield Road, to *Dowding & Plummer*," Roger continues, "but I *did* stress that I could not stand up to do work; as long as I was sitting down I could do a job."

My friend, John Fletcher, was in a very similar situation Roger: he wanted to be a cabinetmaker, but his disability prevented him from doing the job, because he had no choice other than to stand for many hours. He found that *very* frustrating.

"Well they put me on a month's trial and eventually I was there for forty-five years," Roger continues. "I can't say I enjoyed every moment, because there were sometimes problems. Some days you might make a mistake, but I've always taken pride in doing a job well. I enjoyed it for the majority of the time.

"When I met my wife, Jenny, she was able-bodied, but she had health problems later in life. I used to go to my brother's home, which had a pub next door... the *Black Horse*, on the Stratford Road, Sparkhill.

"I'd go drinking with my brother, Terence, (now deceased) who owned the paper shop next door to the pub. I was introduced to Jenny; I knew her Mum and Dad before I knew her.

"We started going out together and Jenny accepted me for who I was (she was seven years younger than me). To Jenny, I wasn't disabled; I was just unfortunately not able! So I really appreciated that – and I've had a wonderful family."

Another aspect of our book, Roger, is the range of degrees of disability, experienced by some of those who are helping us.

You met my friend, Joe McGuire, in the previous chapter. Well he's back again now, to regale you with some further adventures!

Joe remembers: "I got my Invalid Car in 1968. Some time in 1969 I started going to the weekly club: the *Disabled Drivers' Association*.

"There were car rallies in the summer. Those had been going on for some time before I came on the scene. The government took the trikes off the road in 2003," he explains.

I had my first trike in 1958. And here's a photo of an outing to Stourport, with the *Helping Hand Youth Club*. We used to meet at 17 Victoria Road, next to the school. This next photo is you Joe – with a bit more hair!

Joe and I go back a long time. We often went to driving tests and rallies. I'd meet my friends there.

We were at the *Coventry Radiator Company* playing fields, in Coventry, next to the *Phantom Coach*. Roy Cox and Joe came over – and supported me – through some very traumatic times. Roy lived in Halesowen and Joe was in *The Beeches*. They were there to do the driving tests: *Coventry Group* were organising it.

"I first met David when Roy Cox came to *The Beeches* to visit someone else, with Derick Penell; they'd known each other for some time," Joe recalls. "I was introduced to David, with some of the events that we went to.

"Eventually, he started coming to *The Beeches* on a Sunday night. He and Roy Cox would come over then, as a regular thing – for some years.

David, with Joe McGuire, outside Nunnery Road School, where the Worcestershire Sport Club met every Saturday. BY KIND PERMISSION OF JOE MCGUIRE.

"My sister, Mary, made a special cake for me, on a Sunday – and when they came over they'd eat some of it!

"I went to a Physically Able and Handicapped Club, but the one I went to, which David and Roy didn't go to, was the one beside me … at the *Ladywood Centre*.

"In the early days around the beginning of the 1970s, we used to go out quite often, at weekends," Joe continues. "Just out to the country, to get away from the City. We would visit various villages, often around the Bank Holiday; usually somewhere in the Worcester area.

"Then of course, David was the Chair of the *Halesowen & District Club for the Disabled*, at one time, when it was affiliated to the National body. So we paid national subscriptions. Their headquarters were somewhere in Norfolk. People used to go there on holiday, although I never went. Roy and David went on holiday together."

The Centre was in *Ashwellthorpe Hall* – the HQ is still there Joe. Of course, my Trikes were often breaking down – which made it even more difficult. I broke down in the Queensway on one occasion. I was afraid a lorry would come round the corner and crash into the back of me! That was around 5.30pm… in the Rush Hour.

It happened when they were developing the Queensway. There used to be traffic lights at the end of Bromsgrove Street into the Bristol Road. And they built this underpass. I was travelling along there in the snow at 5.30 and came up the other side at the traffic lights at 7.30pm!

I got home to Moseley at 9.30pm. My Trike only had one headlight, like a Cyclops, but I was fortunate that it had a self-starter, rather than a starter handle. I've been rescued a few times but the *AA* and the *RAC*, generally-speaking, didn't want anything to do with my type of vehicle, at that time.

In theory the garage, Ashley Repairs of Hay Mills had a 24-hour service. If you were lucky the bloke came out, but at other times you just had to cadge a lift and leave your car where it was!

I was a nervous wreck, but I've always been like that: I live on my nerves! I got stuck in the swing doors at the *Grand Hotel* on one occasion – but was extricated eventually.

Joe McGuire and I have a history of events: we went to a church service at Charlwalton, which was a church in the middle of a field, near Daventry. They opened up the church especially for us – and it smelt all musty and horrible! Then the vicar came in. The villagers weren't too happy – because they didn't like walking across a ploughed field, to the church.

The vicar just welcomed us – then carried on as normal. Afterwards, we went down to the village hall, where we were given tea. That was quite hazardous for us, because we had to go near piggeries and farm animals; one of our number, picked up some of it on his fingernail, and was none too happy: it didn't mix with his sandwiches!

After Charlwalton, we had a week, every other week, going to places like Derby, for driving tests – or to Stoke-on-Trent. This would start in the summer months.

Joe recalls: "Those rallies would have been in the early 1970s, because I didn't get a car until 1968."

It began with our driving around looking for clues, but then they became more like rallies. We went to Derby, Ashton-under-Lyme, Stoke, Halesowen and Worcester. The Trikes faded out in 2003, but these rallies finished a long time before that, because there were less and less people going to them.

One was held in Sutton Park – I won that one!

Halesowen held theirs in the Button Factory, which smelt terrible, because they used cow's bits-and-pieces, to make the buttons... it put you off your dinner.

I've stayed at some fairly grim hotels, in my time. There was one in particular where if you *looked* at anything, it fell apart and the only thing that worked was the lift!

Joe recalls: "*The Disabled Drivers Association (DDA)* used to arrange an annual outing to a Sports Ground in Bourton-on-the-Water, off the A45. They gave us the concession to park on the Green. We were down there every year, on the first Sunday in August. A nice pleasant atmosphere.

"There *were* parking problems, however, at various hotels and theatres; sometimes there were only two or three disabled parking slots for the Trikes. In one example they took our vehicles away, then brought them back when a show had finished.

"The last time we went to Bourton-on-the-Water, the policeman who normally let us park our Trikes on the grass was no longer there. The Council Leader, was a very irate woman! She berated us and called us all sorts of names... wanted to get us arrested. Fortunately, somebody got in touch with the policeman, so he came over and sorted it out for us," Joe concludes.

Chapter Five

1960s – 1976
The Barretts of Sylvia Avenue

The 'Swinging Sixties' saw the launch of the first Polaris-armed nuclear-powered submarine, the USA's 'George Washington'… and women in that same country were introduced to 'the Pill', for the very first time.

Queen Elizabeth II gave birth to Prince Andrew and the leader of the women's suffragette movement, Sylvia Pankhurst, died. In the field of music, two popular songs of that year were Johnny Mathis' 'The Shadow of Your Smile' and Jim Reeves recording of 'He'll Have To Go'.

Film audiences were treated to 'I'm Alright Jack', with sterling, stereotypical performances from Ian Carmichael and Peter Sellers… in direct contrast to Stanley Kubrick's iconic 'Spartacus', starring Kirk Douglas.

Three couples have played a significant part in my life: Peter and Mavis Barrett, Brian and Lily Filkin and Mary and John Fletcher.

Peter and Mavis Barrett (née Norah Taylor) were supportive in a number of ways. Peter was Volunteer Leader of the Carlson House Scout Group. They founded and ran the *Helping Hand Youth Club*. Peter had met me in the Woodlands Hospital, many years ago, when he had polio.

The hut in Vicarage Road was enlarged, to make room for the various activities. The couple then became Welfare Officers and also founded the *Pathfinders* for 21 plus members. On Wednesday nights they ran the *Adventurers*, for those with more severe mental difficulties. They also organized many social events, such as Barnes Close. I got on really well with them.

Mavis was awarded the MBE in 1971, for services to the *MSA*, over three decades. The Barrett's work was recognized, not only by the children they helped, but within academic circles.

Brian and Lily Filkin were both Quaker fundraisers, raising substantial funding for the *MSA*. Brian lived opposite my grandparents' nursery. He bought a rose for every year of his marriage, from my grandfather's nursery! Brian and Lily also helped to market products, which had been made by the Disabled.

They had a bungalow in Birmingham, housing the *Rick Sue Trust*. Lily helped to organize the pre-school disabled children from the Nursery Unit, who were later transferred to the main school.

In 1976, when it looked as though they were going to do away with the Trikes (aka 'Puddle Jumpers'), I decided to take driving lessons with BSM.

The proposal to ban Trikes, involved myself and a group of sixty others lobbying Westminster Hall, or the Houses of Parliament. That happened in 1976.

They finally banned Trikes in 1996, so it took 26 years before that came into effect. Every July, when Parliament was about to Recess, they always announced something that couldn't be talked about, or dealt with in Parliament. Following constant lobbying by organisations like the *Disabled Drivers Association* (*DDA*) – and the fact that every motor racing driver who had an accident was hauled up and asked to drive the three-wheeled Trikes, which had evolved from vehicles, following the Second World War, and were rather primitive and unreliable, to say the least!

The balance on them was fairly good, but they were very unreliable due to faulty engines and exhausts that broke off. These were Villiers 2-stroke 197 detuned Go-Kart engines. However, going back to the racing drivers, trying them out, they always said that the Trikes were dangerous.

But I wouldn't agree with that. A motorbike of itself isn't dangerous, but its safety depends upon the skills of the driver. You have a metal chassis, with a fibreglass body, on the Trikes. So despite the fact that they were deemed dangerous, very few people were killed in one. One person was killed, but he was taking passengers – and they'd come back from a drinking spree – and he was killed. But one of the prime things on the dashboard said, 'No passengers to be carried'. So he was breaking the law on two counts.

As far as I'm aware, there was no concrete evidence that Trikes caused accidents. The only thing was, that they had space at the driver's side, for a folded manual wheelchair – so you had a bit of space there. In a Tippen for example, you had a seat that pulled down, which was quite handy if you wanted to go up to the Clent Hills – it was called the Snogging Stool!

I actually had the experience, but one had to be careful not to get caught up in a ploughed field, and not be able to get away, because it was only a one-wheel drive! But enough about my first wife!

So they announced in July 1976 that they were going to phase out the Trike, because it was dangerous. At this stage, Minis were available for disabled people with children up to the age of fourteen. But when the child reached that age many had to be given back. That was as it stood. So people were up-in-arms about the prospect of losing a Trike.

We started off lobbying, as one did in those days, in Birmingham City, by going on a Saturday and driving slowly through the centre of Town, holding up all the traffic!

We then went down to London, having written to our MP, a Mr Litterick. So I went with John and Mary Fletcher and we had to fight our way through the Anti-Abortion Lobby. As we did so, I explained to them that if they had their way, there'd be more of us – not less! We were a group of about sixty people, from all over the country, representing the *Disabled Motorists Association*.

When we entered Westminster Hall, some of our group were walking on sticks and crutches and needed somewhere to sit down. But they were not allowed to have a chair, in case they attacked the MP with it! I'd written to my MP on several occasions, but his agent, Mr Albert Bore, wrote back saying, "Please do not write to him again on this subject. He is far too ill."

Going back to Westminster Hall all of these people in our group handed in a piece of paper, and then the MP came down and greeted you.

I attached myself to John and Mary Fletcher, who live in Tamworth, Staffs, and their MP was a Mr Grocott. So the MP came down and the Conservatives said that they weren't getting rid of the Trikes, if it had anything to do with them.

They then held a Party Political Broadcast over our heads, saying, "Oh I didn't know about that – I'll have to look into it!" So it wasn't really satisfactory and that day I personally learned that Democracy is not very good at all.

John, Mary and I were invited to have a cup of tea with John Grocott, their MP; there were steps everywhere and no ramps. John recalls that particular day:

"We took David down with us in the car. There was a hall full of several hundred disabled people, but only about fifty chairs, when we arrived – and we had to wait."

The reason for the shortage of chairs John, was to prevent them being used as missiles!

"Yes – that we might be riotous! We had to wait for a long time, then eventually we saw our own local MP. We were quite lucky, because David wasn't able to see his."

Mary explains, "Our MP was quite nice and he did speak to us, although it didn't make an awful lot of difference, but we thought we should do our bit. I think he was a Labour MP. We've all had the experience of trikes breaking down and so on. At the moment we're just a little more able," adds Mary.

Jim Callaghan had just taken over from Harold Wilson, when we lobbied Parliament, but they actually kept Trikes for a few more years, so maybe it did some good? At one time I used to drive myself all over the place.

Anyway we got back and home and subsequently, the nurses went on strike. We joined them on a picket line, in the *St John's Hotel*, Solihull. The police were very helpful: while they were showing us around the car park at the back, David Ennals, the Minister of Health, walked in the hotel, from the front!

Mary Fletcher's view of her education at Carlson House, with hindsight, differs from my own.

"At the time, I didn't realise. It wasn't until I left school and started to work and do other things, that I realised that it wasn't as 'up-to-scratch' as it probably should have been.

"Some of the other pupils took GCEs and so forth – I personally didn't. I didn't feel that I was encouraged to do that – for whatever reason... I've never really got to the bottom of that. We had to have a certain amount of intelligence, but I was never offered the chance to take any exams, or encouraged to reach that stage," Mary remembers.

"On leaving school, I worked at *Dyas Development*. It was a local firm in Perry Barr. I had some switchboard training before I left school, so I got a job on the Switchboard at *Dyas*. I'm sure they're not there now. I worked there for about six weeks, and then the Managing Director said that I wasn't suitable for the job; but he didn't tell me – he told my Dad! He hadn't even got the guts to tell me.

"But what I haven't told you is that I was very shy as a child – and I think that affected much of what happened in my childhood. My husband, John, met David through the *DDA*."

"That's right, Mary and I met at the *DDA* and then David started to go there as well. We had an immediate rapport between the three of us, so we got to know one another, over a period of time, in the early 1970s," John recalls.

"It was especially apparent as well, when David met Maureen Pritchard, his second wife; we all got together, as a foursome. They used to come to our house, for a meal, in Tamworth, Staffordshire. We've lived there for forty-six years.

"When I left school I wanted to be a cabinet maker," John continues, "but under the company rules that applied then, I had to stand at the workbench for eight hours a day.

"After six months, I was no longer able to do that. The able-bodied men could cope with it, but I couldn't."

So both Mary and John were unable to continue with their first jobs. I suppose they weren't such enlightened times then – people didn't understand the needs of the disabled.

"Yes, one thing that has changed for the better, is that they couldn't do that nowadays: they couldn't say that we have to leave because of our disability. They are obliged, by law, to have a certain percentage of disabled employees on their staff, but it depends on how disabled people are," observes Mary.

"I was a very late walker: I started at about three-and-a-half. The doctor referred me to the hospital and I had to wear calipers. I carried on living with those and having the Mickey taken out of me," John recalls. "Children can be very cruel can't they?

"But, on the positive side, I went to both Junior and Secondary schools – mainstream. When we had Games Lessons I took part as best as I could; the teachers had a good understanding of my needs," John explains. "Because I was fairly strong I was always the 'Tug' at the end of a tug-of-war! I could weightlift as well, more than anybody.

"I managed to keep up with the rest, academically, but I had a twelve-month gap between Junior and Senior School, so, age-wise, I was twelve months ahead of everybody else.

"We have two daughters – Amanda and Heather. They are both delightful: very helpful and over a number of years they've given us four grandchildren, as well, who are the 'light of our lives'.

"So we've been able to lead a normal family life, which, with many disabled, is not the case," John observes.

"Yes, we've also been lucky enough to start a sports club," interjects Mary. "From that we've managed to go abroad, to France and Germany – to our twin town of Bad Laasphe – in Germany. We went to the sports club there and met disabled people, who were doing sports activities. We had quite a lot of fun doing all of that. We were called *The Terriers*.

"But ourselves, we've been to Spain and places like that. For our Thirtieth Wedding Anniversary we went to America, to see a friend of ours. We went on our own and we had a wonderful time!"

John recalls, "We started being involved with Sport in 1978 and we finished in 2005, when I had my stroke."

"Those years were wonderful," remembers Mary. "Not only did we run a sports club, but we also had a swimming club as well. Personally, I was much more involved with the swimming – and enjoyed it very much."

"Also, we ran a Support/Advice Group for the Disabled, which Mary was involved in, to a great extent."

"Have you ever heard of *DIAL*? Well, we were similar to that – which was a telephone advisory service, but we also had people coming to an office in Tamworth. We gave them advice on various things; we helped train ourselves and all sorts of things – we did that for twenty years. We helped a substantial number of people during that time.

"But then, unfortunately, the funding ran out. We got sponsorship and all sorts; it wasn't government funded. John was the Treasurer."

"Yes, I was always told off, for not giving enough money out. But the local council used to give us funding; they realized how useful we were. Had they had to employ people to do the same job, it would have been far more expensive for them, so they paid the room hire for us and we worked for free.

"After trying to be a cabinet maker, I became an Estimator in the Plumbing & Heating business. I'd always wanted to work with my hands rather than my head, but because of being disabled for thirty-five years, I had to work with my head. And because of an accident, when I was eighteen, I had Epilepsy.

"Due to the pressure, we decided as a family, that I should retire in the late 1980s, but we carried on doing all of these extra things," John explains.

"We had quite a busy life, until quite recently. We got to know lots of different people and various societies, during that time. We counselled people too," recalls Mary.

"Mainly it was disabled people who weren't getting enough money and couldn't cope, so we would point them in the right direction, their local MPs and so forth. A lot of the people we helped trusted us, because we were disabled ourselves and had that experience in common.

"It doesn't necessarily mean that you know how another disabled person feels, because you're talking about different degrees of it," she continues. "Because they could relate to us, they automatically thought that we could relate to them! But the fact that we were there for them was important; we provided a very good service.

"Nowadays they have to go to the *Citizens Advice Bureau*; they do have specialised people to help, but not to the extent that we were," Mary concludes.

I first met Tina Hackett through the *MSA* where she was a Physio. Maureen had a lot more to do with the *MSA*, when she used to go there, but Tina will give you more precise information.

Tina, would you begin by describing the work that you did at Carlson House, between 1977 and 1980?

"I started as a Paediatric Physio; ever since I qualified I wanted to work with children. So the chance to work locally to where I lived, with a particular group of children, was a dream really. I was living in Harborne and was very close to the Centre and to the school.

"There was one other Physio and we worked together – eventually becoming friends. Our remit was to assess and give treatment to all the children in the school who needed it. We also had an Orthopaedic Consultant Clinic at the school.

"They had two fulltime Physios within the school system, with maybe a hundred pupils. They also had teachers, teaching assistants; House Mothers who were there to change the children and to help move them around the school, attending to their daily needs; but they also helped at Lunchtime," Tina explains.

When the school opened there were only around 32 pupils. Last year marked the 70th Anniversary of its opening.

"One of us would 'man' a Lunchtime, helping to feed the children, which was part of the treatment: management of them to help them with feeding and to help them feed themselves," Tina continues.

"There were a very wide range of disabilities when I worked there, because the basic criteria of the school was that the children had to have cerebral palsy; they also had to be of normal or above normal intelligence; they were very much chosen for their intellectual ability. Physically, we had an enormous range.

"We used to assess the children, then put them into groups; we'd work with those groups and also with individual children, during the day. So again, there were the House Mothers. There was also a Porter who was responsible for building maintenance, sorting out the wheelchairs and doing some of the gardening. We were in converted stables, at the bottom of the garden; so there was a covered walkway between the main house and the Physio Department.

"So we'd do the assessment; the treatment, work with the groups; help at Lunchtime. We'd also help whilst the children were being loaded onto buses: another opportunity to help children who needed walking and climbing practice."

I remember a climbing frame in the garden, where Carlson Park apartments now stand, Tina. In my day the Consultant visited weekly, every Thursday.

"We'd run the Clinic for the Consultant during his monthly visits; often we'd refer the children to him, if we had a particular concern David," Tina continues. "There was Mr Innes, who was the first; then Alistair Thompson took over. We worked with the children; did Home Visits during the school holidays; we would also do Hospital Visits. If any of our children were in hospital for an operation we would visit them: talk to the Hospital Physios; worked out exactly what had happened; make sure that the operation that we thought was happening had happened! Work out what the regime was; work alongside the hospital physios – and also with parents."

Alistair Thompson later established a back and hip replacement clinic in Edgbaston.

"The amount of time they were in hospital would vary considerably, from a few days: less than a week was the average; we did have children who were in for longer: if something hadn't quite gone right or if the child had had an unexpected seizure; they might have had a reaction to an anaesthetic; or just the fact that they'd had an infection. Those children may then have been in hospital for longer," Tina concludes.

Chapter Six

1967 – 2000
Life with Maureen

Maureen was just lovely. Her cerebral palsy was more profound, in the sense that she had a severe speech impediment and always had to carry a handkerchief. There's a guy named Paul, who lives in Harborne; he's been a lifelong friend of mine. He's maybe a few years younger than David. Paul married Annette, who is very similar to Maureen.

I remember Paul saying to me, "Annette and I complement each other. Because I'm the brains and she's the pair of hands!" Now I'm not suggesting that that was the same with Maureen and David. Annette agreed with what Paul was saying – she wasn't offended. She'd say, "Paul makes sure we've got food on the table – and I make sure it's cooked!"

You sometimes find that quite a lot, with people who are mutually disabled.

Peter Millington

This is a photo of my first marriage to Maureen; myself and Roger Robinson. She was Maureen née Harris. It was at Halesowen Church.

We were married in 1967, for three years, but it only lasted a short while; she had Spinal Bifida. In those days we thought that sex was a number between 5 and 7!

This is my first Trike: one headlight; XDU 58 – a Coventry registration plate (see Chapter 4 photo).

My second wife, by pure coincidence, was also a Maureen... Maureen Pritchard. She was spastic and was more disabled than my first wife – quadriplegic: she could walk about, had regular falls, and she loved water.

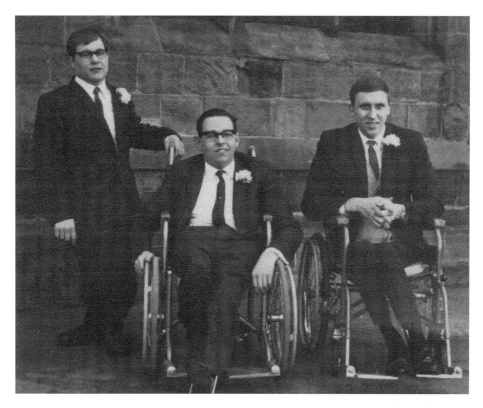

The Three Musketeers: from l-r: Roger Robinson and Roy Cox, with David in the centre. The three friends went everywhere together – hence the title! Taken outside Saint John's Church, Halesowen.

Looking through my album there is a photograph taken next to our maisonette, in 1976 with her Trike and mine.

Another photo in this collection was taken in the *Jane Hodge Hotel*, which was opened by Lord Tonypandy (aka George Thomas): a state-of-the-art hotel, just outside Cowbridge, in Wales.

A third photo was taken when we went to Jersey. That was the honeymoon suite, because it was the only one with a double bed. It was at *Maison de Londes*, St Ouen.

We met at Carlson House: we went to school together: she was six and I was twelve. Maureen cried every time she left her Mum. She had a saliva problem, so she was always carrying a handkerchief.

We had a Carlson House School Reunion in 1997, John and Mary Fletcher, whom you're going to meet again in this chapter, organised it, together with Maureen and me. We tried to contact all of the former pupils, but most of them didn't want to come!

When we were at school Maureen called me a "Big-headed Big Boy"!

She went to riding stables for the Disabled, with the *MSA/CPM* and they were all led round by helpers there. But Maureen was more proficient than that, so it was agreed that she would go to a farm in Worcestershire, in Inkberrow. It's where *The Archers* programme was based. The pub there is the *Bull's Head*.

So she went to this farm in Inkberrow every Wednesday and got on a horse that went a bit – which Maureen liked. But if it got 'spooked' it would try to get rid of her. So she fell off the horse and fell onto her arm, which appeared to have produced arthritis – that was the start of that. This got progressively worse.

Maureen was always plagued by frustration. The part of her brain that was affected by being spastic, was better if she had a drink... she could always do more if she had a drink; she was more active and she could walk in a straight line.

As her mind was very active she had difficulty in sleeping. She took Diazepam, but only in moments of emergency. If she was having dental treatment she *had* to be knocked out, because otherwise she'd bite the dentist – and wouldn't let go!

She learnt how to control her tongue... most women can't! She had to lash her tongue behind her tooth, but then the tooth went rotten and she had to have it out.

Maureen's Trike, decorated for the wedding, during her Hen Party at the MSA Centre. She drove it back, in all its glory, to her home in Thirlmere Drive, off Wake Green Road, Birmingham, near Sarehole Mill!

There was nowhere she could go to have her teeth straightened out, not even the Dental Hospital – so that was another worry.

Gradually she deteriorated and therefore drank more. The condition got a lot worse and she was in a lot of pain. I've never doubted that was the case – I don't doubt it now – but her family would not accept this.

It was suggested by Tina Hackett that Maureen might go into a wheelchair, because she hyperextended when she walked: to save her legs for a bit longer. But her mother and sister wouldn't accept that (her father had died by this stage). They said that Maureen was being lazy. So they both went to the *MSA/CPM*, where the situation was explained to them.

Roger Robinson recalls: "In the case of Maureen Number One – she and David were quite happy together, at first. I was the Best Man at their wedding. She found it difficult to cope with David. I'm different because I keep my thoughts to myself, but if I have to say something I certainly will!

"But it's different when you've got time to think. Sometimes you say something and you think: 'I shouldn't have said that!'"

In the event, Roger, once we'd parted, it took from 1970–1974 to resolve everything!

"Maureen Number Two was a very nice person," Roger continues. "She was unable to speak clearly and that used to make her frustrated. She would give an opinion and David would translate, because sometimes you couldn't understand what she was saying. She became very depressed because of the frustration of not being able to speak. But the two of them looked after each other. I used to visit them quite often.

"People with disabilities do tend to think that others think they can't do anything – but that is wrong. They say that young kids can be cruel, but as a disabled person you need to show people that, although you may be disabled, in other ways you can cope.

"When people ask, 'Does she take sugar?' You just have to ignore that kind of attitude, because you are who you are," Roger observes.

Jane Hall came to look after Maureen, from *Goldsborough Care Company*, which was arranged by Social Services. Jane had been a nurse and had a young daughter, who was at St Martin's. She decided that she wanted to earn a few bob, so she came to assist Maureen getting up in the morning – having a bath et cetera. Other duties included taking Maureen out to lunch; shopping; driving out to various pubs; or maybe cooking lunch at home.

Maureen and I moved to Monastery Drive in 1995... we first met Jane the following year. She came to the house, several days a week, to help Maureen get up and have a bath. Sometimes she'd prepare food for us; she's still doing it for me now – once a week, at the moment, possibly twice.

Jane was born in Hong Kong, so if you turn her up-side-down it says,

Maureen and David's Wedding Day, 10 September 1977. Taken in the garden of Heronfield House, Chadwick End.

'Made in Hong Kong'! Her father worked for *BOAC*: he had a good job with them out there – a Bentley car and all the rest. The family were seconded to Egypt. They lived in a range of countries, so Jane had a very interesting up-bringing. They had servants. Jane's Mum came out to get her baby, James, but somebody had taken the baby and the pram from the veranda. They found the baby in the gutter, but the thief had gone off with the pram! As a result of that her brother became quite poorly, so it was decided that they would return to England.

Most of her family eventually left Egypt, but the Airport Authorities wouldn't let her father out. She describes what subsequently happened, later in this chapter.

I spent my first Honeymoon, with the first Maureen (née Harris) in 1967, at the *Arundel*, having spent the previous night at the *Grand Hotel*, Birmingham. We travelled in our separate Trikes, as they only carried one person.

I remember a man in dark glasses, coming in and giving us our breakfast in bed! And all that business! We went to the *Arundel* several times.

When Maureen decided to leave me, we were booked to go to Denmark, with some other Trike drivers from around the country. My friend, Norman Healey, from Bromsgrove, looked after me and we became firm friends.

We stayed at *Hans Kanutz Platz*, which was opposite the Tivoli Gardens.

I knew Norman through the *Disabled Drivers Association*. He was a poor young man with tuberculosis. He went to Kunzles, the cake people's place in Davos, Switzerland, to try to recover – a lot of people did.

Norman and I took a young lady there with us, who was in a Trike. We stopped at Odense, but we couldn't get into the toilets! The doors were in the way; a man arrived, who just happened to be there at the time. He lifted the doors off their hinges for us. He was from *Stour Valley Trucks*, Stourbridge.

We stayed there for a few nights and then we went from Odense (where Hans Christian Andersen was born), on the ferry, to Copenhagen.

We were met in Copenhagen by the disabled people. We were coming down this dual carriageway and turned left. One lady in our party, whose name was

Holiday in Denmark: postcard showing various tourist attractions.

Hilda, did a U-turn, in front of the traffic! I was following a Mini. We were following each other in a set order.

The Mini went over some traffic lights, at 45 miles per hour, which I couldn't do. So I got cut off: I was holding on for grim death! Bear in mind that I was on the wrong side of the road!

We eventually got to *Hans Kanutz Platz*. It was the forerunner of *The Beeches* in Birmingham really. *The Beeches* was modelled on that: everybody had a flat; then if they wanted nursing assistance they rang the bell. *The Beeches* was at Six Ways, behind the old Children's Hospital.

Anyway, we stayed there, but we were only sleeping on the settee and if you tried to shut the window it dropped off! Being on the tenth floor, if the window was open, it sounded like Paddington Station in the Rush Hour!

One of the young ladies with a Mini – 'Slender Brenda from Hull', was rather keen on Norman and asked him if he would go off in her Mini. But Norman stayed with me and we did our own thing – which annoyed the ladies greatly!

However, we persevered and we stayed in Copenhagen. You looked over a wall and saw the diminutive figure of the Little Mermaid. It's only little!

We went out to the Disabled – and had a meal which lasted for ever. It was a buffet, laid out on the table – it took all afternoon! That was an experience. The Danish people, at that time, had a great thing about privacy. So they were interested in our vehicles, but they wouldn't come over and speak to you, unless you called them over and said, "Would you like to look?"

There was no dirt on the ground and no radios blaring because that was impairing your personal privacy. But they called the Germans 'The scum of Europe', because they were taken over by them. So that was Denmark.

Norman and I arranged other holidays with two women – Hilda and Elsie.

We also went round the Lake District – and to Lake Coniston, where Donald Campbell died in 1967. It was the 50th Anniversary last year. We went to the hotel that he stayed in and there was the door – all the way along the wall. There was also a Memorial Stone.

They said that they never found his body but one of the racing engineers from *Lucas's* said that although they didn't find his body, his head was up a tree! They didn't recover his boat until decades later. So that was quite eerie!

We started off at the *Moota Motel* in Cockermouth; we also went to Grasmere and visited a Beatrix Potter landmark. If you approach Windermere from a certain angle, you can just see it lying back. The film about her had me in tears. I can't stand injustice, so the film upset me greatly. It was actually filmed in Ireland!

I can't really put any dates on this, but we probably had two holidays a year, with Norman and the two girls. We met up with Gwen later, whom Norman eventually married. We went to Ayr on two occasions and Largs, which is a little bit further up... on the Clyde Estuary. That was as far as we could drive, with

Culzean Castle, Ayrshire, Scotland. Following the holiday in Denmark and the trip to the Lake District with Norman Healey, the four of them went up to the Marine Court Hotel, in Ayrshire, for a couple of years, followed by the holidays in Largs. They were surprised to learn that General Eisenhower lived in the castle, post-war. He had a lift installed, so that he could access every floor.

two days solid driving. We stopped overnight. We could only average about 35 – 40mph. It was hard going!

Two elderly spinster ladies ran the *Marine Hotel*, in Ayr. In Largs we toured a place that belonged to the Electricity Board.

I visited the Isle of Wight on several occasions with Roy Cox of Halesowen, whom I originally met at the *Helping Hand Youth Club*. You may recall, from a previous chapter, that when you were 21 you left and joined the *Pathfinders*. I didn't do that as I'd met the first Maureen by that time.

I was also trying to initiate an affair around the same time, with letters in the *Disability Now* magazine... *Lonely Hearts*. I met a girl on the Isle of Wight. That was a bit embarrassing, because I had to get rid of Roy! I didn't tell him I'd met this girl – she was fairly disabled.

Sadly, Roy is dead now: we were known as the *Three Musketeers*!

In the film that my Biographer, Shirley, and I watched together, *Steps to Independence*, Paul Johnson of *The Archers*, (who lived not far from here), is doing the commentary on it. I bought a budgerigar from him for 2/6d. The bloody cage was 12 pounds! That was one of the things I gave to my wife – even though she didn't want it!

I returned to the Isle of Wight while I was going out with the second Maureen. The lady in the Isle of Wight was quite keen on me, but she lived too far away.

I had met Maureen who lived just down the road from me, in Thirlmere Drive, which is on the opposite side to Sarehole Mill.

So I started taking Maureen Pritchard out – I took her to the Birmingham Group of the *Disabled Drivers Association*. When I introduced her to people they looked at her as if: 'Ooh heck!' I didn't want to embarrass her, so I took her along, but I didn't really go with her as a couple; didn't really talk to her that much. She never forgave me for that, but she didn't understand that I was embarrassed, because she was another Maureen!

We eventually overcame that. The first time I took her out, we went to the Pictures – the Scala, on the Smallbrook Ringway. Parking was a bit difficult so we went onto the pavement. Maureen ran up the steps and the stairs and left me, sitting at the bottom! But I got up there somehow.

I thought: 'I'll get my own back!' So I said to her, "Go and ask that usher for an ice-cream." Well of course she wouldn't because of her speech defect. So we sort of went from there.

We met at the *Birmingham Boat Show* really. The *MSA* used to have a stand there – at Bingley Hall. They raised money, as the 'Friends of the MSA'.

We were quite well matched because we came from the same background and the same education: we were both at Carlson House School.

So we started going out together, but I could hardly understand a word she said... so life was a bit difficult. As she had never been allowed to go out anywhere, she was ashamed to be seen in public places. Well I didn't like that view at all: if people stared, well good luck to them!

She was quite attractive on that photo that I showed you – she was twenty-six then. For ages we used to go out for a meal, but Maureen never ate much. We'd go to places like the *Hung Do* in Five Ways. We had a curry there once and she kept looking up to the ceiling. I wondered what she was looking at, but it was the only way that she could keep food in her mouth!

A middle-aged chap came over and said that he'd won on the horses and would we allow him to pay for our meal? I said, "That's very nice of you. We'd have had more if we'd have known!"

Joe and I also went to the *Hung Do*, which fronted onto the Hagley Road. We'd go up the pavement at the back. There was a pub up on the roof.

Roy and I enjoyed going the Odeon New Street to see people like James Last. I saw Johnny Cash; the Everley Brothers and Roy Orbison. Although there was a big area at the back, by the *Tavern in the Town* only three Trikes were allowed to park and they'd still get the bloomin' Fire Brigade. You had to be lifted up two steps, then they'd take the wheelchairs away: you'd sit there wondering if they'd bring them back – or if somebody would pinch them!

We were still sitting there once, when the ushers came to clean the place up. We said we were waiting for the next performance. They said that was in the morning, so we said that was all right!

We also went to the Gaumont to see *It's a Mad, Mad, Mad, Mad World*. We went to the pictures a lot in Stourbridge, because we could get in free. Sometimes we'd go two or three times a week. But bear in mind that I had to drive from Stourbridge to Bournville, over Frankley Beeches, in the dead of night. If a clutch or throttle had broken I'd have been stuck up there – before the days of mobile phones.

Roy had a young lady friend called Jean, who considered herself to be superior. The first time that Maureen (my first wife), Roy and I went to the West End, we went up to Jean, but she hadn't got her makeup on and we didn't even recognise her! She thought she was 'superior – to all inferior!'

Going back to the second Maureen, when the Jehovah's Witnesses came I'd say: "Well if my wife hadn't had a blood transfusion she'd be dead by now. Goodbye – thanks" ...got rid of them very quickly!

On our honeymoon we stayed at the *Wychbold Hotel*, opposite the Droitwich Spa overnight and then we went to the Severn Valley Railway on a foggy day.... Here's our marriage certificate below:

We came back; did the shopping in Bromsgrove.

She used to call herself 'Second Hand Rose'. Our holidays were restricted to how far Maureen could drive. We went down to Lyndhurst in the New Forest and we also went over to the Isle of Wight, which we drove around. Once again

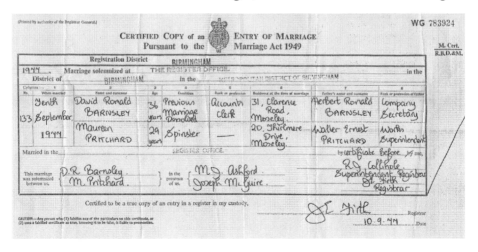

Their Wedding Certificate.

I was in a 'muck sweat', because Maureen's ignition light came on. As we drove around we were thinking that it could conk out at any moment!

For all of these trips, we were all in our own individual Trikes.

I knew where the garage was on the Isle of Wight, so we went there and it was just a loose wire. We got back on the ferry. Maureen drove quite slowly after that. On the way back I had no indicators, so I wanted to rush back to get to Ashley's before four o'clock, to get it fixed. I left Maureen in Stow-on-the-Wold, plodding her way back.

By the time Ashley's had fixed the indicators Maureen was back. But she was ill, so I got a dressing down from her mother: "You always take her away – and she always comes back ill!"

But, short of wrapping her up in cotton wool, I don't know what else I could have done!

You may recall that Jane Hall first met Maureen and me around 1996, the year after we moved into Monastery Drive, Solihull. She was helping us on a daily basis, during the week and on every other Sunday.

Jane explains: "I was helping Maureen. I'd go in in the morning, make a cup of tea, then she would have a bubble bath. I'd help her in and out of the bath; sometimes comb her hair. So ... getting her up in the morning, into the wheelchair.

"We'd have breakfast; I'd fluff the bed up; put the washing out.

"Sometimes we'd go out into Solihull. Maureen liked shopping – she liked spending money! She was very interested in clothes; always impeccably dressed. We'd maybe have coffee out, come back. If I didn't do brunch/lunch then somebody would come in for the afternoon. Maureen enjoyed sitting in the sun. I'd help take her to the toilet – all sorts of personal care.

"Sometimes we'd go out on a Sunday; if not I would cook a Sunday Lunch. Again, just all general care for Maureen; no housework or anything like that. The cleaning lady came in to do that.

"On other occasions we went to the *Arrow Mill* and had a nice lunch there: that's out Studley-Evesham way, in the countryside," Jane continues. "Then there was the *Golden Cross* and the *Dog*. David would be driving. He had a very nice Honda; then he had a Volvo. He could drive us and get in and out of the car, with a bit of effort: he had very strong arm muscles.

"Maureen's wheelchair would be put in the back and she was able to transfer into the car; she could walk a little bit. She had an extended walking style – putting her legs right out in front.

"She'd have a sherry, have lunch and then come back. Sometimes we'd go out in the week too – for a trip around the shops; David would go off and do what he wanted to do; Maureen and I did what she wanted to do.

"They liked driving around and looking at the countryside – just getting out of the house really. It was nice – we'd go to lots of different places.

"David mentioned earlier that I was born in Hong Kong. Then we moved to Bermuda, Egypt, Macclesfield, followed by Wilmslow. My Dad became a manager at Birmingham Airport, so we moved to Solihull.

"I trained as a nurse and went to East Birmingham Hospital; then worked at the Priory Hospital in Edgbaston, in the cardio-thoracic unit. I left there after I had my daughter, returning to the bank staff for a little while, working part-time.

"Maureen was a very intelligent woman who was locked in a disabled body. It was very frustrating for her all the time," Jane continues. "Her speech was also a problem, but once you got used to it, you could understand some of what she said. She was a very funny lady, but some of the things she came out with – to people who were being ignorant with her!

"She had very good 'one-liners' – some of which are unrepeatable – *most* of them are unrepeatable. She was good fun; she admired a nice gentleman – no harm in window shopping!"

If she'd had her way Jane, she'd probably have run off with someone!

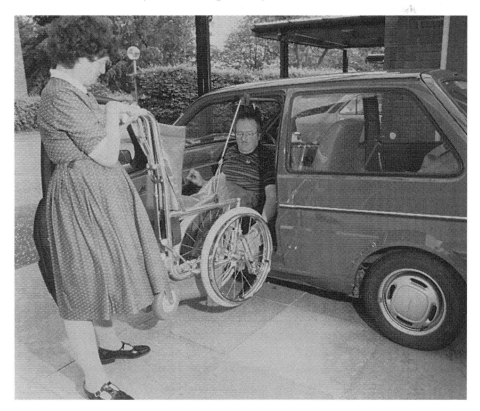

Maureen helps David into his first car, a Metro, outside their bungalow, on 205 Harborne Park Road.

"Absolutely David! Of course, as I got to know her more and as she got older, she became more depressed. She was focused on herself and her problems, so she became more insular.

"Maureen enjoyed horse riding – she did that for a long time – and when she died all of that money went to Riding for the Disabled. She just enjoyed the freedom of being able to move – and the freedom of movement that the horse gave her."

Shirley likens Maureen's situation to Anna Sewell, writing the novel *Black Beauty*. Anna was bedridden for most of her life, but through her novel she could imagine the freedom that her horse characters experienced. Wishful thinking really, because she wanted to be free like her horses.

"Yes, I think Maureen would have been a real 'Go-getter', if she'd been an able-bodied person; nothing would have stopped her! She'd have gone out and shone really. She was very popular as a person. There was nothing she couldn't have done, given different circumstances," comments Jane.

"There's a photo of her, sitting in the front row of children at Carlson House. She was six years younger than David.

"I didn't actually accompany them on any of the holidays; other people helped them with that," Jane concludes.

Joe McGuire recalls our Driving Tests and Rallies, at the *Coventry Radiator Playing Fields*, next to the *Phantom Coach* depot:

"We were doing some Wheelchair Racing there, but it didn't go very well over a field!" he explains. "One of the chaps Johnny Welsh (he's dead now) was a little chap of a diminutive size. He said, 'I'll give you a good chase!' But I didn't realise, a soft field… I got through – but rather slowly! We used to do that quite often – it was a bit of fun!

"As far as helping David is concerned, I wasn't aware that he was in trouble, until we went over. The first time I got an inkling of what was happening was when we were on our way down to Worcester, with Roy Cox. It was the old A38 at the time and we were coming down that hill, towards the Chateau Impney.

"Roy was in the front and I was behind. Next thing I saw this Trike in my mirror – and it was David, going at a fair lick, coming to the very front of the line. That was completely out of character for him.

"When we reached Worcester I asked Roy, 'What's the matter with him?! Normally he'd hang back behind a car and he wouldn't pass it.'

"It was only after that that I realised that the first Maureen had gone."

Thanks Joe. I first met Jenny Willock, in 1995, when she answered an advert in the paper. I wanted an 'Enabler' for my wife and I, to try to make life as normal as possible.

According to Jenny, "Prior to that, I'd worked for *BT* for a substantial number of years, but I wanted a job that made a difference to somebody – that if I wasn't there, I'd be missed. Raj was at the interview too, at Dave and Maureen's. Dave and I got on immediately; Maureen wasn't quite so keen, at first, because I wasn't able to understand her speech impediment; whereas Raj could do that. I never quite tuned into her and I think that frustrated Maureen," continues Jenny.

"But we got on and had a laugh and in the summer I used to do a bit of gardening. David would go out with a cup of tea and I'd go out and start messing about. Maureen would come barging out: 'I'm paying you to look after me!' She didn't like me chatting with David – she liked to be involved.

"After Maureen had passed on, I still helped David," Jenny continues. "We'd be out shopping and David would need some money. If I'd got his bag he'd say, 'Mother – can I have me money?!' He'd introduce me:

'This is my Carer – but she doesn't care!' That always used to produce a chuckle!

"If we were out for a meal we'd just sit there like any ordinary couple, but you could see people looking at us, thinking: 'I wonder what their relationship is… what's going on there?'

"Different people, over the years, would say to us, 'Oh, how long have you two been married?' Dave was always quick to say, 'Oh we're not – we're not married!' I was inclined to let that go on – let them keep guessing. I'd say things like, 'We're not married – we're just living together.' Or, 'David's been married for twenty-five years and I've been married for twenty-three!' To baffle them.

"But instead of laughing with us, people would just look at us: 'What have you got to laugh about?' It was strange."

One of the points that Jane Hall made to Shirley, when they were discussing what improvements have been made for disabled people, over the years was that, to some extent, we still need to educate the public; because they sometimes still treat disabled people as though they were from another planet!

But I also think that it may be because when they see someone who is different to themselves it can be a bit un-nerving, so they react in a self-protective way, because they don't really understand – a kind of defence mechanism.

"Although that's the opposite of what we found, in some cases," Jenny remarks. "A lot of people would come and chat to us, to find out what was going on. They tended to think that people in a wheelchair were deaf!

"It always depended on what Maureen wanted to do on a particular day. For example if she wanted to go out for lunch, the first thing was to decide where she wanted to go. So we'd make our minds up and set off. Then she'd say, 'I don't want to go there.' So there'd be screeching tyres.

"Then we'd go shopping for clothes. David used to drive, on those occasions and then look around the shops. But Maureen absolutely loved her clothes. There was a dress shop in Knowle that she loved. She wore two-pieces: like a loose buttoned-up top and a pleated skirt. But she did have some lovely clothes. We'd shop at *Beatties* too, in Solihull or Sutton Coldfield," continues Jenny.

"We'd drive out into the countryside, to have a meal. The *Rose & Crown* at Portway was one she particularly enjoyed… it was the nearest that we went to. On one occasion it was just Dave and myself. He'd got this remote access control on his truck. We were sitting in the window, just about to leave and there were two old ladies walking down the road, in the same direction that his vehicle was pointing.

"Dave pressed his Remote and opened the car. I said, 'You're wicked you are!' So the back of his vehicle just opened up, as they were walking past! But he loves anything like that – he's got the devil in him… maybe we have a similar sense of humour.

"As Maureen was in constant pain; any painkillers she took made her ill, so the only pain relief she got was the sherry. It did work – but it took a lot of it, to work. She drank it in a mug, without a handle on, so that would shorten the process.

"Although she could be quite moody, she was also funny and witty: when you got there in the morning – and make jokes and things. You always used to say that Maureen didn't like me Dave, but actually, we did get on.

"When we went to the *Rose & Crown* at Portway, we had to go up a road and over a little bridge, then right. As we went down this hill, we always had to watch the traffic, coming from the left. Dave would say the same every time: so I'd be sitting in the back and Maureen at the front.

"As we went down the hill Maureen would start to laugh. Dave would say, 'What are you laughing at?' 'Nothing!' Then he'd say, 'I've got to watch the traffic.' But every time he didn't know that I was prodding her! She was just cheeky.

"She loved horse riding. She felt normal, riding a horse.

"She also enjoyed going swimming. I'm not even sure if she could swim, but she just loved being in the water. She used swimming aids… and loved the water going over her head; it was similar when she was having a bath.

"I actually stopped helping Maureen after about three years or so," recalls Jenny, "because she started to get more demanding and crafty.

"I was caught between her and my loyalty to Dave. You *did* have to do what she said – there was no arguing – you'd do it!"

My wife was an interesting personality, because, as Joe and others have said, had she been an able-bodied person, she would probably have gone far, with whatever she chose to do; a very determined and intelligent person, but trapped in that body; it was so frustrating!

"Yes, she was an intelligent, quick-witted woman – and I imagine she loved life – before she got too disabled. She loved men."

"She used to type letters for Edgar, the Workshop Manager at the *MSA*, didn't she Dave? You had a gnome in the garden at Monastery Drive, which she named after him! She'd say, 'I'll go down the garden and see Edgar!'"

I could tune in to Maureen, so people would sometimes have to ask me what she had said. Shirley had a similar experience with a young boy with cerebral palsy. She was his Maths and English tutor for quite some time. Sometimes she could understand him by relying heavily upon context, but at other times she had to ask his mother.

"I felt a failure, as I'd spent a lot of time with her, but still couldn't tune into her," Jenny continues. "Because when you're helping someone, you're trying to make that connection aren't you?

"However, we *did* have a connection: something would be said, or we'd just look at each other and make eye contact and have a giggle. There were very few in-depth conversations," Jenny concludes.

Pete Willock, Jenny's husband, recalls:

"The first time that I met Maureen and Dave was when Jen asked me to take them out to Christmas Lunch, at the *Malt Shovel*, Barford. Jen was an Enabler then – with the wheelchairs. I paid for lunch to repay the fact that they bought Jen lunch, every time they went out.

"There were things at their bungalow – like general handyman jobs, I did those. Dave could drive himself then, but eventually had to give up.

"Between the ages of seventy and seventy-five he gradually wound down. He's only got one working eye and he was struggling to keep awake. So if they went out for a meal, at lunchtimes, he was suffering on the way back.

"He then had to change vehicles, so that he had a vehicle where he would go in the back and have a driver in the front," Pete concludes.

My friend, Mary Fletcher, comments: "When we went out with David and Maureen, over the years, to various pubs, we used to have quite a good time. We'd also go to a club that has already been mentioned several times – the *DDA*. We've had some really nice times with him and Maureen – we really enjoyed it.

"Since Maureen died," Mary continues, "David's been over to us at Christmas time and out with us with the *Terriers*; we've had some really nice get-togethers.

"When Maureen was twenty-one, although she had great difficulty in talking, she stood up at her twenty-first birthday party, on the stage and thanked everybody... in front of all of her relatives and friends. It took a lot of doing – because it was so difficult," Mary continues.

"She met Princess Anne. Maureen was full of life and full of energy, but became very frustrated, because she couldn't express herself, in the way that she would have liked to."

That Pebble Mill programme, during which she met Princess Anne was about *Horse Riding for the Disabled*, Mary. It was also about the opening of Carlson Park, which replaced the school.

"Had she not been so handicapped, she had enough innate ability to really make something of herself," Mary adds.

"Yes, communication was her weakest point, if it hadn't been for that, then her life would have been completely different. She would have communicated with David better as well," interjects Mary's husband, John.

"Mind you, if she really wanted to say something to you, she would. If she wasn't happy with something, or if David spoke for her, but didn't get it quite right, she would make sure that people got the message!" adds Mary.

Chapter Seven

Climb Every Mountain (Holidays from the UK to the Exotic)

The 1980s began with the British Government granting permission for a private consortium to construct the Channel Tunnel. Queen Juliana of the Netherlands abdicated in favour of Crown Princess Beatrix – and the musical, 'Les Miserables', was first performed, at the Palais de Sports, Paris.

The Education Act of 1981 placed new duties upon local education authorities to integrate children with special educational needs into mainstream schools, along the lines suggested by the Warnock Report of 1978.

An IRA bomb exploded at the Grand Hotel in Brighton, during the Conservative Party Conference of 1984, killing and injuring some of those present… Margaret Thatcher had a narrow escape.

Maureen and I embarked on a series of holidays, through the 1980s. We used to go to Jersey – to the *Maison De Londes*. Maureen originally holidayed there, back in 1967, having been sponsored by the *Spastic Society* (*SCOPE*). So she went on the first of those. We went there all through the 80s up until 1999. We lived for our holidays!

The *Jane Hodge Hotel* was part of John Groome's organisation. It was built in the Year of the Disabled, 1981, when Maureen actually went to Buckingham Palace, to be presented to the Queen, at a Garden Party. It was something to do with the *MSA* now the *CPM*. She went, but I wasn't invited. Maureen was very smart – always loved her clothes, but it rained all day and she got absolutely soaked! The Royalty were in a tent, but the others weren't. That was one of her moments of fame, together with meeting Princess Anne, which I told you about in an earlier chapter.

Jenny comments: "When Maureen and David stayed at the *Jane Hodge Hotel*, in Cardiff; they had happier times there, when they'd got each other. But David's solo holidays, or when people have gone with him to help him, haven't really been that successful."

We also found a guesthouse called the *Haven* in Hay-on-Wye, so we used to go and stay a bit; it's this side of the Brecon Beacons – sometimes combining this with a visit to Maureen's family at Ystalyfera – twenty-three miles this side of Swansea.

We'd been with the same tour company to Spain, Costa del Rada, twice; we also visited Malta... Sliema. And we went over to Gozo. The truck that belonged to the Disabled had broken down and they couldn't get a replacement. So we travelled in old vans and put the wheelchairs on our laps. As we were driving along, the back of the truck used to open up!

We went to a place where the Mediterranean lapped over the road. The driver pulled up and we did a 360 degree turn! That was on Malta – it wasn't very safe. They used to take police cadets to help us as part of their training.

The last time we went to Spain the leader of the party planned to be there over a period of several weeks. We were in the second batch; when we arrived

The Haven Country Guest House, Hay-on-Wye.

we asked for somebody to help us with getting on and off the coach – and what-have-you. But it appeared that the first coach had not arrived from England, and the leader of the party didn't appear until 12 noon, with a 17-year-old police cadet. It transpired that, allegedly, they were 'having it away'! We were none too happy, because nothing had been organised. The long-and-the-short of it was that we were all getting back to the tour company, saying, "What the heck?"

For the second week they sent out a coach. One of the previous party had appendicitis so he was staying in hospital. The leader of the party had gone back on the plane with the police cadet, using the hospitalised man's ticket. So I wrote to the Chief Constable and to the tour company concerned, saying what a fiasco it had been. The Chief Constable wanted more details, so I held back at that point.

Later on, we went down to the *Mobility Road Show* in Reading and one of the police cadets was there! I asked: "Are the police cadets still helping the tour company?" He said they weren't, but that wasn't the end of it.

One of our more exotic destinations was Hawaii. My Biographer, Shirley and her husband David, visited Kauai and Maui, but that was a huge journey, even for relatively able-bodied people!

Jenny Willock recalls: "I wasn't around at that time, but I heard about how dreadful the journey was. Maureen couldn't get to the toilet on the plane, and

A postcard of Hawaii, Waikiki Beach, Honolulu.

Lake District: the Ravenglass and Eskdale Railway.

they arrived in the early hours, wondering what on earth they'd got themselves into!

"David likened their hotel to a brothel! With all the sailors. And the heat – Maureen was ill – she got bronchitis. I think they came back from it, wishing that they'd never gone. It was way too adventurous – but she was fifty... she wanted to do something special. One of the highlights was a visit to Pearl Harbour," Jenny continues. "Dave does like his holidays but it's very rare, as far as I know, that they worked out happily."

Aside from these holidays, I enjoyed going to the countryside, various places around the West Midlands and a bit further away, with the *National Trust*. I particularly liked going to Chatsworth, which you can never take in, all in one go.

Also *Blenheim, Osborne House*, on the Isle of Wight – all of that is of interest to me, because I'm very keen on History. I'm a member of the *Severn Valley Railway Trust*. I was there, right at the beginning; lapsed my membership for a few years, but now I'm back. I went on a *Flying Scotsman meets the Tornado* event, in 2016.

I've always been keen on motor racing; not today's motor racing, which I consider to be extremely boring. But in the 1960s we used to go to Silverstone, (near Banbury); to Mallory Park and a few other places. We'd get there at 9 o'clock in the morning, staying in the centre of the circuit for the remainder of the day, whilst the racing was taking place.

So this is still the 1960s. Stirling Moss, is a particular hero of mine; I was devastated when he had his big crash, at Aintree. He didn't just race one car – he was in every flippin' race that was going! Possibly the first professional racing driver in the UK – and the first celebrity in the business too.

He was the only person who didn't win a championship: he actually gave it, through the rules, to Mike Hawthorn, who subsequently died on a bypass in a Jaguar.

I also enjoyed the Big Bands and the shows. We were frequent visitors to the shows at the *Birmingham Rep*, but I'm not going now.... I've seen most of the things that interest me. My musical tastes are bands, Roy Orbison, Duke Ellington; Count Basie – not necessarily at the same time!

I don't know why I like Big Bands – I just do. I follow the Syd Lawrence Orchestra now, which is run by Chris Dean: he bought the rights.

According to Shirley, Alton Douglas enjoys the big bands too. He played trombone in his own Quartet at one time. She co-wrote his biography, *The Original Alton Douglas*, with him.

We met Raj Bartlett, when Maureen and I interviewed her in 1991; Barbara Brand and Tina Hackett were there too. It was at the *MSA* in Harborne.

Raj recalls: "I went for a second interview at Maureen and David's home in Harborne Park Road. It was a warden-controlled bungalow. I was nineteen at that time; I'm forty-five now.

"It was Maureen that I was being employed by, so I was concentrating on her, because she was the person who I had to impress. Before I went for the Harborne interview I read a book about how to behave at interviews, so I sat up with my back straight and spoke directly to Maureen – eye-to-eye contact; shook her hand firmly and so on.

"Then when I went for the second interview at their house. David came across as really caring – full of joy. I couldn't believe that someone with that many disabilities could look on the bright side!

"David was asking the questions, although Maureen had already told David what she wanted to know. But when I answered the questions I spoke back to both of them. I took a friend with me, Sharon, because I was really nervous; I had no previous experience of that kind of job, but I needed to do something."

Maureen got so frustrated when people didn't understand her; they tried to talk for her or finish her sentences. They didn't have the patience to give her time to answer, as Jenny explained in an earlier chapter.

Raj continues: "I'm much younger, so my way of dealing with anything like that is to say, "Maureen, have you got something to say to the lady?" Then she'd stick her finger up, but I was just as annoyed as Maureen was, although I had a childish way of dealing with it, as a youngster, because I had fire in my belly all the time!

"A man stopped us at the traffic lights," Raj recalls. "Me and Maureen were walking up Harborne High Street and we were crossing the road. This man, grabbed Maureen's hand like this – and he put something in it, closed it and said, 'For you!' I said to Maureen, 'How rude can people be? He's just patted you on the head! Do you *look* like a dog?' I'd say it really loud, to try to embarrass that person. He'd given her a sweet, so I said, 'Chuck it at him Maureen!'

"But usually we would make a joke out of it; otherwise, things like that would really be upsetting. We'd encounter things like that, all day long."

The relationship between Maureen and yourself, was that there were no 'airs and graces' between you Raj. How exactly did that work?

"Well, first of all, my language: I swear a lot – I still do... as she did. When she was about to swear I just looked in her eyes – and I knew she was going to.

"But she was a bit more sensible than me: she wouldn't do it with a stranger: she was very well-mannered and very well brought up. But her family all thought that they were something that they weren't! Although Maureen was brought up by them, she never thought of herself as being bigger or better than anybody else," Raj continues.

"Sometimes she'd just wear clothes a couple of times. It got difficult towards the end, because she had an inverted hernia; she got bigger and bigger; then the alcohol made it worse. So shopping became more embarrassing for her. When I first came on the scene she was a size 10 or 12.

"She was a pretty woman, but she went from that to almost 18/22. So it was no longer fun to go shopping. Maureen became worse as she got older, she started drinking more, to try to block it all out.

"She started grinding her teeth too: they would all have had to come out eventually, and she'd go on liquidized food. Her knees would start giving way a lot more; whereas before she'd be in the wheelchair, in the house, but she could still walk around, holding onto things, all of that stopped.

"When she walked she extended her legs; instead of there being a bump where your knee is, they'd go back. Everything just became difficult.

"She had a very lively mind and an adventurous personality, but she was trapped inside a disabled body – so frustrating. That's where David came in, you see? Whatever Maureen wanted or needed, David made it possible. So if she wanted to go somewhere where wheelchair access wasn't possible, or some other problem, David would get on the phone and arrange it.

"If she wanted to go on holiday, David would get on the phone and sort it out. If there was a complaint to be made somewhere, David would make the complaint.

"He was her voice, her eyes, her ears, her transport," Raj explains. "He would lead her into something that maybe she didn't want to do. She didn't need courage or confidence, but physically, she couldn't do it. So he made it possible practically, for her to do it.

"Sometimes she'd phone me on a Sunday, when David wasn't there, but generally-speaking she couldn't make phone calls, because people couldn't understand what she was saying. So he made the calls for her."

"Eventually, Maureen's disability became too much for her and she turned to alcohol, to ease her pain and suffering.

"David carried Maureen, but Maureen, emotionally, carried David," continues Raj. "She was the stronger of the two – emotionally. He was the stronger of the two when it came to practicality and logistics. But emotionally, she was very intelligent. Even though she employed me and Anne, who was my co-worker at the time, we did twenty hours each a week; so although she hired and fired us and paid us, she made sure that we looked after David too."

Maureen got jealous sometimes, if she thought Carers were spending too much time with me. But maybe that's understandable, because in her situation she was so dependent upon Jenny and Raj.

"This is where I think Maureen could have held back sometimes," observes Raj. "When she was upset it came out nasty, especially when she was jealous. For example, she was worried when we went to Hawaii that because she was in a plaster she couldn't do as much as she'd have liked. I was concerned that David needed to enjoy his holiday too. So we went on a trip one day, leaving Wendy and Maureen at the resort. We had a fantastic day: we had giggles, we had laughs. But the more I went on about it, the more annoyed she got.

"But I thought: 'Tough! The truth is Maureen you got drunk and you fell over. It's your fault, not David's.' And that's how I used to talk to her.

"When Maureen actually died, the official Coroner's Verdict was 'Asphyxiation', because she'd fallen forward into a cushion, when she was on the toilet. But she couldn't get herself back up.

"But I was happy for her – because she was out of her misery. What was left for Maureen? I know she had David – but what did Maureen have for Maureen? Nothing. It's a bitter-sweet story.

"David still had his voice... and Maureen didn't. Her worst fear was to be left behind, without David. Because her family would have taken over completely," Raj continues.

"They even blamed David for her death. They said that he should have poured the drink down the sink. I said, 'Excuse me, don't you dare come in here, picking on David. Have you ever tried doing that with Maureen? Have you ever tried to tell Maureen that she can't do something? Because you'll know about it! Yet you come here criticizing David. David did his best.'

"But they just walked away. It was mainly the alcohol to be honest. She was always a big drinker, from the time I came to help her; initially, giving her a drink when I arrived was part of our routine, but it just got worse.

"It was so difficult, because I knew I was going against David. And I loved Maureen and David equally – they were like my Mum and Dad. But what could I do?

"She would say to me, 'I pay you.' And I'd say, 'Yes you do.'

"I stopped working for her in 1997; so I worked for her for about six years. But we stayed friends. I never lost touch with Maureen and David."

There's no doubt that you made a significant difference to our lives Raj.

"Being young, I probably brought fresh ideas; a different perspective on life. A new perspective on Race. At first you probably thought I was going to be this girl who'd never been out on the streets – and whose Mum didn't drink. But there I was, in all my glory, smoking and drinking. I had a boyfriend: all the things you might never expect of a young Asian girl! So I opened your eyes to that, but mainly I think what you're talking about David, is that I enabled you to do things."

Moving on to holidays Raj, there are three that I'd like us to talk about: Lanzarote, Hawaii and then Switzerland. For most of these holidays abroad it was usually with you.

"When we went to Lanzarote I'd never been abroad before, apart from India. I was absolutely flabbergasted that Maureen and David could book holidays, get on a plane and ensure that the wheelchairs were there," Raj recalls.

"David organised everything; he took care of all the paperwork, all the finances; I just remained the Enabler. I enabled Maureen to do what she wanted to do.

"When we got there, the Complex was lovely. The three of us had such a laugh! We all had wine and packed lunches, but Maureen fancied herself as a bit of a Porn-type person!

"She fancied the captain, in this photo (opposite), and she was drooling all over the place! But when I took another photo of another lady, almost sitting on David's lap, she got jealous. I was new at the time and Lanzarote was my first holiday with them, this was in 1995/6.

"This second photo (opposite), is David and Maureen on board the same boat, same day. They had giggles and laughs together. She had a hanky all of the time.

"We went back to the restaurant at the resort: the food was lovely and so were the staff. It was very calm and there was no bad atmosphere between David and Maureen. They'd been to Lanzarote before so they knew what to expect, but I didn't. It was really easy: they felt comfortable; they weren't nervous. We didn't fly over on the same 'plane. We met when we got there," explains Raj.

In Majorca we met up again with Anthony and Joan, renewing our friendship, after many years apart. We stayed at the Norwegian Holiday Home, which was

CASAS HEDDY - LANZAROTE

Casas Heddy, Lanzarote.

Left: *"Hello Sailor!" Maureen with the catamaran skipper, in Lanzarote. BY KIND PERMISSION OF RAJ BARRETT. Above: 'Poles apart!' Maureen and David, on the same boat trip. BY KIND PERMISSION OF RAJ BARRETT.*

normally strictly for Norwegians. But Anthony and Joan had become friendly with them, so we were allowed to go and we had quite an enjoyable time there.

We went on a bus, which was supposed to have a commentary – a Guided Tour, but I think it was semi-broken at the time – rather like the hotel that I told you about – where the only thing that worked was the lift! We enjoyed going into Palma and doing a bit of shopping. We also went out on a catamaran.

At Lanzarote we stayed in chalets and there again, we were with Anthony and Joan. We hired a taxi to go around the island, on a day trip.

"This is my photograph of Anthony, Pippa, Maureen and Joan, also in Lanzarote," Raj continues.

"When Anthony talked he used his hands a lot. Maureen didn't – she couldn't be bothered. She could have achieved at a higher level, like Anthony did, but I think she decided she was quite happy as she was, as David's wife.

"Anthony and Maureen knew what each other was saying.... I knew what they were saying as well. Anthony's speech was a lot clearer than Maureen's, but when they were drunk, they were as bad as each other! He and Maureen had disabilities in common. The photo was taken in the restaurant area of the hotel," remembers Raj.

"I love this photo of the Fancy Dress Party (opposite) – especially of David. He's really enjoying himself isn't he? It was the last night of the holiday. They couldn't stop laughing because David couldn't believe that we'd got him to dress up! I said, 'Come on Dave!' He didn't really want to, but he found it so funny, because Maureen was laughing at him. That was a really 'fun' holiday.

"The whole hotel was adapted for disabled people, so if there's an able-bodied person in any of the photos it's because they were a helper. It was run by the Red Cross. We bought Maureen some new trainers, because her feet were swelling up. This next photo is of Hawaii. Unfortunately Maureen broke her leg before we went there, which David was really p***** off about! Things were going from bad to worse by then. That was probably one of the worst holidays that they've ever had.

"Maureen didn't want to go: she loved water so much, but she wasn't able to go in it, because of the plaster. Then there was the journey on the aeroplane – an 18-hour flight. I was working for them on the holiday, but back in England I was now living in Leicester.

"I told them I didn't need to be paid, because I was a friend of theirs; just pay for my ticket. But they said, 'We're paying Wendy, so we're paying you, so that's your spending money for your holiday.'

"I took most of the photos; if I'm in the picture, it was probably taken by a waiter or waitress," Raj explains.

"I photographed a visit to another hotel, because the hotel they were staying at didn't have a pool.

Late Night Fancy Dress Party in Lanzarote: the Sheik of Arabee, with concubine.
BY KIND PERMISSION OF RAJ BARRETT.

"Maureen and David were really disappointed when they arrived at their hotel, at 4am; it was more or less like a whorehouse! The sailors and other blokes were waiting downstairs and we would have to go out for breakfast. So the whole time that we stayed there it was purely for sleeping. But because it was an *Outrigger Hotel* we could use the facilities of any other *Outrigger Hotel*: they were dotted everywhere.

The particular hotel that we decided to use was on Waikiki Beach; that's why they're looking so happy!" Raj observes.

"More of my photos were taken on a cruise ship: nothing extravagant – just a tour around the island. It was in November. Wendy was the other helper. This other man was the guy who organized the actual holiday – he seemed to be a bit of a rogue! He's the one who didn't tell us that the hotel we were staying in didn't have a swimming pool!

"He was there for himself – not for anybody else. Just before this holiday David had lost his Mum, in May 1996. He was already grieving for her, so anything that went wrong seemed even worse than it actually was.

"Also, Maureen did nothing but drink on that holiday," Raj recalls, "because she couldn't go in the water; she couldn't do anything fantastic, because of her leg being in plaster.

"I have a photo of a helicopter flight, from Oahu, which was part of an excursion, to the Main Island of Hawaii, to see the volcano. We couldn't go near it, on foot, because of the wheelchairs. I went so far, but it was very rocky. But we could see it from the helicopter, as we flew over. We could see the steam and the lava flowing.

"From the minute David and I left the hotel, we had fun and jokes. But when we told Maureen about it when we got back, she said, 'Yes, well I'm glad you had fun, while I was stuck here with her' – (meaning Wendy).

"Because all Wendy wanted to do was sunbathe or sit in their room and read books. You see if I'd have stayed back with Maureen, we'd have been in the pub!" observes Raj. "I think the mistake I made was coming back and going on about it!"

When we went to Malta we had to be at Heathrow to be put on the 'plane first. Then the rest of the passengers got on. The airline apologised for the delay, but they'd had some rather awkward baggage to take on board – (the disabled)!

When we were about to take off, the 'plane stopped, because it had some electrical problems. So we sat in the 'plane 'til about one or two o'clock in the afternoon, then because of the time factor, we had to wait for a change of crew! We took off and we arrived, in Malta, and eventually arrived in Sliema about five o'clock. When we got there, bearing in mind we'd been sitting on the plane for all that time, without going to the toilet, I was absolutely desperate to go!

On arriving at the hotel, we were confronted with a flight of steps, but luckily we went round a corner and in through a gate at the side – and into the hotel. What a relief – literally!

In the middle of the night there was a heck of a bang: the tyre on my wheelchair had punctured. So I had to try to get that fixed. Whenever we went away it was like a military operation! I had tyre tubes, levers and all that business, but couldn't do it myself. So one of the Voluntary Police Cadets helped me – and we went from there.

One of the comments that Jenny made was how persistent I was, with our holidays. She said that if she'd had to sort out all of the logistics that I had to resolve – she probably wouldn't bother!

But, you see, I had another problem: I used to speak to Maureen and say, "Would you like to go here?" "Oh yes, yes, yes!"

Then two days or so before we were about to go, she'd change her mind… she didn't want to go. This was extremely frustrating and very difficult. But she also had other problems at this time. We went, but it was not a happy time. One of the police cadets had claustrophobia, on the flight to Malta. He was quite a nice chap. He told us that although he was a policeman, he might have to go down a hole or something! Luckily on the way out it didn't manifest itself, but it became more of a problem on the way back. I think because he was tired – but luckily he didn't throw himself out of the 'plane … and us with him!

The police cadets were there to assist with lifting on and off – coaches and what-have-you. One particular person claimed this police cadet, all the time he sat in a wheelchair. But when we were leaving, he stood up, folded the wheelchair – and walked onto the 'plane! Now this was to the detriment of other people in the party – and that was typical of the behaviour of *some* disabled people. It can give us, as a community, a very bad name.

There was no excuse for him, because Maureen and I managed the best we could, but we were limited, by her walking ability and various other things – so we needed that extra assistance. We were grateful for the assistance we had, but in practice these things don't always work out as you've planned.

The Maltese people were absolutely wonderful and made us feel very welcome. They loved the British. Mr Mintoff, who's just about taken power again, didn't like anybody who had a uniform. This couple, who we were in contact with for a couple of years afterwards, offered to put us up for six weeks, if we could find the fare. We were very keen on this, but discovered that some of the amenities available in Malta itself, were very basic, for example, the hole in the ground!

To complete the holiday list, let's look at Dartmouth. Maureen's sister and brother-in-law, had an upside-down house in Street. It was their holiday home. We stayed at the *Dart Marina Hotel* in Dartmouth and went on the boat, up to Totnes and back again, visiting various places of interest, such as where the Dimblebys lived; Agatha Christie (aka Mary Westmacott) also had a place there, which was quite interesting.

We visited a place where the Normandy landings were practised. There was a tank there, on the left, on the sand. We drove around, but Dartmouth was very difficult for parking. We went to Salcombe in my Metro car, but it wasn't very good up hills: I was afraid of being trapped in Salcombe – and not being able to get out.

The Lake District we've done, Cockermouth and so on. I also stayed at Bowness on Lake Windermere. I went to Grasmere, the first time we visited, but when Maureen and I were married, we went to the Lake District several times.

When my father died, in 1986, we took my mother to the *Baron's Court Hotel*, which is where you turn left from Windermere, to go to Coniston. But I got into more trouble – because my mother had diverticulitis and was very concerned about taking her Fibergel. Maureen felt I thought more of my mother than I thought of her. It was all right for her to eye up any bloke in trousers!

Jenny was straight – and truthful. Maureen's drinking problem caused a rift, because Maureen asked for a drink, when I was out of sight. But I think a lot of Jenny – I might tell you.

Moving on to my favourite holiday – a trip to Switzerland... and who was organising the party? The same company we'd had problems with before! The owner came as well, with his 'bit-of-stuff'. He'd booked the best room, for him and

Lake District – Dove Cottage.

his 'floosy', but one of our party was severely disabled and had nowhere to go, so he had to go into that room and the couple moved out! This poor chap owned several Estate Agents. He was a very large bloke, who'd had to pay extra for his seat. Following a bit-of-a-stroke, all he could say was, "No, no," and "Yes, yes."

Happily, during that holiday we could just go out of the hotel and on to the boat. So, ironically, it turned out to be the best holiday I ever had!

Also, I met up with some friends that I'd known years ago – Chris Addis (she's dead now) and her husband. They lived by the *Lodge Hotel* in Solihull Lodge. Furthermore, I was reunited with Vera Dean, a disabled lady, whom I first met at the *Arundel Hotel*, in 1963.

She'd written about her experiences when she'd been in a home for Spastics: many were put in homes – which they stayed in almost all their lives, becoming institutionalised. It broke my heart the first time I saw it.

Vera later wrote about our Swiss holiday, including the following holiday itinerary, which we have paraphrased:

She and her friend, Gladys, like ourselves, set out on the holiday on 6 August 2007 and they soon met up with our group of 24 other disabled people. The two ladies became friendly with five particular members of our group: Sid and Chris; Stuart, who was in a wheelchair, but lived life to the full – and Raj and myself.

We took off for Zurich at 12 noon and after a short flight, departed for Weggis, where we reached the *Post Hotel*, around 6pm. The hotel overlooked the scenic shores of Lake Lucerne. For some reason the hotel food for our group was substandard, so Vera and Gladys ate out in self-service cafes.

Vera recalls that every morning, after continental breakfast, she and Gladys enjoyed the orchestral music, being played on the lake shore. They took a steamer trip every day, which had wheelchair access. The ship stopped at all the villages and small towns.

Vera describes the city of Lucerne as 'a very grey, old place with buildings going back hundreds of years,' but adds that there were ultra-modern buildings along the lake shore.

"Yes, Maureen had long gone by then. David said he needed a holiday, so I said I'd go with him – to Lucerne – which is a big town," Raj explains. "Wheelchair access to the main buildings was 'spot on'. We didn't encounter any trouble, apart from the fact that they kept wanting to tip David upwards, rather than forward!"

Following a long walk around Lucerne, plus shopping, we returned to Weggis for a meal in the hotel. Later that evening, Vera, Gladys, Stuart, Raj and I met for a drink. It was Gladys' birthday the following day, so I ordered drinks all round; everyone in the café serenaded her with Happy Birthday. According to Vera:

"... a happy band of people walked back to our hotel that night."

She also describes the steamer trip to Mount Rigi, where we were all lifted into what appeared to be a cattle truck on the mountain trip, to reach the summit 5,900 feet high. The day concluded with cards, birthday cakes and presents, for Gladys, from other group members and a jolly evening in one of the waterfront cafes.

On the Thursday, we returned to Lucerne for a shopping trip, with the rest of the party, followed by a boat trip the morning after, to Fluelen, visiting the quaint little town of Brunnen, on the return journey.

Saturday morning: our group visited Beckenried, taking the cable car to the summit of Mount Klewenalp. That evening some of us missed dinner, to watch an excellent firework display.

Sunday morning: Raj, Stuart and myself accompanied the two ladies to Mount Pilatus. A train took us up 7,000 feet, to the top of the mountain. It's the highest mountain railway in the world – a 40-minute journey.

There were spectacular views from the top, on that hot summer's day: snow-covered peaks for miles around! The railway staff eventually assisted us back to the train. Quite an achievement – reaching the top of Pilatus – when three of us were in wheelchairs!

Raj interjects, "that day we went in a train – at a 45° angle! When we got on, it was already on an incline. So it felt a bit strange, because we were standing upright, but the train was at an angle. I particularly liked it because it's rather symbolic and typical of David's attitude: 'Climb every mountain', that is 'Try everything!'"

Mount Pilatus, Switzerland.

The return trip to the UK was rather stressful, culminating in a Fire Alert on landing – and an evacuation of the airport building!

I always preferred to do something interesting on holiday, not sit on the beach and gawp. I'm quite proud of the fact that I could get about and I've been to many places, including the National Trust. We used to have a lot of day trips and Raj was really instrumental in helping us to do that.

Chapter Eight

Disability Resource Centre and the MSA

It's interesting that whereas many disabled people weren't too keen on the early institution that helped them, but glad to get out later into the workplace, David's life experience seems to have been the other way around.

'At the age of 62 he was becoming reflective about his life as a disabled person. In many ways a lot changed in society since he was born in 1941 and, in this 2 part series of short biographical articles, David has shared some of his memories as well as some of the photos from his remarkable historical collection. The article provides a chronological framework of David's life.'

Pete Millington

Shirley found Pete's 2-part interview with me, on the *CP Midlands* website. The *CPM* Headquarters are next to the site occupied by Carlson School. The site is now called Carlson Park, opened by Princess Anne in 1986: an apartment development.

Pete is now a Service Manager, at the *Disability Resource Centre*, in Mackadown Lane. He taped the article when I visited him at *Prospect Hall* Selly Oak in 2003. I was 62 years of age at the time of the interview and was living in Monastery Drive. Photos accompanying the article were scanned from an album that I loaned to *CP Midlands*.

He later used extracts from the articles in his book. In Paragraphs 3-5 inclusive he quotes my words verbatim, within speech marks.

Shirley subsequently interviewed Pete, at the *Disability Resource Centre*, for this book. Pete and Tina Hackett, both experts in their respective fields, share the remainder of this chapter between them. Their words are shown within two opening sets of speech marks and a closing set.

"I first met David when I was working as a Care Assistant, on a holiday for Disabled Adults and their Carers. It was run by the *Crossroads* organisation... a big Carers Organisation in Birmingham," Pete recalls.

"It was originally set up by Roger Tongue, the actor who played Sandy Richardson, in the *Crossroads* TV programme. He eventually died of leukemia, but was a wheelchair user in the series.

When I was eighteen, I didn't have a clue what I was going to do, as a career. My Mum and Dad suggested that I went into nursing. I wanted to do Mental Health Nursing and I was accepted at an interview, at Hollymoor Hospital. But I was steered towards doing General Nursing.

I trained as a Nurse, between 1979 and 1982, at Dudley Road Hospital, as it was called then; it's now City Hospital. I was in a group of thirty young women, which was very nice! I was one of only three male nurses, so it was quite unusual, at the time. There are many more these days.

It was quite a complicated course, covering all aspects of nursing.

But I was very interested in Disability. I did some voluntary work, when I was about sixteen, at a Residential Home in Halesowen, for people with Learning Disabilities. We used to take them up to the Clent Hills, and on holidays. I was always very engaged in that sort of work: I got a lot back from working with Disabled People – and I still do, to this day!

I started doing Voluntary Work for an organisation called *Birmingham Phab Camps* ... an Integration Charity, which took able-bodied children and disabled children away on holidays together, so that everything would be shared and they'd all muck in together.

Back in those days, there were no disabled children in mainstream schools. It was great for the able-bodied kids, because they had to slow things down and modify their behaviour. The disabled kids were mixing with their able-bodied peers – something they never experienced at school.

It was a normal educational environment, but there were no pressures – it was a holiday! So that got me into disability issues. I went back into the General Health Service, in *Hillcrest*, which was at Moseley Hall Hospital. We helped people with 'acquired disabilities' – people who had become disabled later in life. So, people with things like strokes, accidents, spinal injuries; multiple sclerosis, ranging from 18 – 60 years of age. It was called a *Young Disabled Unit*, but catered for a wide range of ages.

The difference there that I found, with working with people with acquired disabilities, was that those people had had a certain identity before their injuries: they had jobs and they remembered what life had been like pre-injury. So for them it was a very negative experience, because they'd lost their identity and their ability to do things; lost their power and control in the family. They'd gone from being the breadwinner to being the person who had to be helped. So there was a lot of frustration tied up in all of that.

I had experience of people becoming very depressed. It was a psychological battle as much as a physical one. The National Health Service didn't recognize the importance of the two factors at that time – it was more about giving intensive therapy to people and getting them out of doors. But when they went home they were met by this wall of 'What do I do now? Four walls – I can't get out of the house!'

Whereas I very often found that adults who had been disabled since birth had a very different psychology, because their identity had always been to be a disabled person. Ok – there might still be resentments, but those were often more to do with the environment: 'Why can't I get into the library? Or do this job? You've trained me and educated me, but now, nowhere is accessible.'

There was a Three-House situation: *Brays* in Sheldon; *Wilfred Stuart* in Erdington and *Victoria School*, in Northfield.

In the late 1980s I worked for *Crossroads* – and met up with Dave – on a holiday.

It was great – it was in a hotel, on the seafront. It was a very mixed group of people. Most had brought their own Carers, but there were about five us who were there as Floating Carers, to give the regular Carers a bit of respite and support. There were probably 30+ people in the whole group.

The Disabled people brought their own relative, or partner. There was one chap: I'm not sure if he was the Carer, but he was sixty-six and his Mum was eighty something! But he was running around in his Trainers as if he was a young kid – very interesting!

There were probably about six of us who worked for *Crossroads*, so there were about 15 patients, each with his Carer (30) – plus us. 35 in all, so 1-1-, plus 6 extra.

There were no medical facilities – it was a normal hotel... probably three-star: we did have to 'manage'. But it was a great week. We spent a lot of time in the local pubs, in Teignmouth.

I was a bit overwhelmed by David, when I first met him. I sat at a table, at mealtimes, very close to where he and Maureen were. He's a man who talks a lot, in quite a loud voice – quite often! But he's very pleasant with it. He doesn't 'mince his words'! Which is great – it's very refreshing. And he's very inquisitive: he likes to find things out; he loves Projects – to stimulate his mind.

He asks quite searching questions and he forms opinions about things... that are often strong, but are worth listening to. You might not always agree with where he's coming from, but his ideas are quite thought-provoking... he challenges things.

Eventually, I came to work at *Disability West Midlands* in the 1990s, but we'd entered the 21st century when I interviewed David. I'd meet up with him occasionally or he'd phone the office for some information, or he might come to our AGMs.

I worked for *Disability West Midlands* for sixteen years: they were based at Moseley Hall Hospital – then they moved to *Prospect Hall* in Selly Oak. My job has always been to give people information and advice, to empower them... make their lives better.

But I've also done a range of things. One of the things that we did was the *Heritage Project*. That involved looking at the World History of disabled individuals. But also the Social History of Disability.

My current employer, *Disability Resource Centre*, was twenty-five years old last year – it was our anniversary. Our first Centre opened in 1992. We were at a place called Bierton Road in Yardley, which was an old school, converted by the City Council, into a Disability Unit. We then moved to these Mackadown Lane premises in 2010. I've been with the *Disability Resource Centre* since 2007.

If people want help from the Centre, we have Information/Advice, plus a whole range of things from People's Benefits to Housing and Independent Living. We run training courses in the centre downstairs, where they can learn about computers; we run *Health and Wellbeing Courses*, which involves gentle exercise; we have a Walking Group; we teach people about their personal safety. If anyone would like help, just phone 0303 040 204.

With regard to my *Disability History Timeline*, (included in this chapter), when I was working at *Disability West Midlands* during the 1990s, it was quite an historic time, because in 1995 the Government introduced the Disability Discrimination Act. That was the first anti-discrimination legislation passed in the UK. It has been altered since then, but 1995 was the key year.

There were a lot of Demonstrations and Protests, leading up to the passing of that legislation. At that time I thought it would be interesting to start marking down some of the key events in the journey to that landmark. And also things that happened afterwards. I've borrowed from other people's research too; it's certainly not all my own original research.

A Timeline of Disability History after the Industrial Revolution

Pre-1740s	Before the industrial revolution people with impairments lived in rural communities sometimes subject to poor laws and local charity.
Late-1700s	Rural hardship, swift urbanisation and mass industrialisation affected poorer people with impairment who become increasingly excluded.

Early-1800s	Era of philanthropy and state intervention – the large-scale founding of workhouses, hospitals, asylums and charitable institutions.
Late 1800s	Institutionalisation was the dominant State response to disability in towns and cities.
1890s	Development of eugenicist science affected political, economic and medical policy.
1900s	Strengthening of the working class union movement included early disability rights groups.
1914-1918	The Great War created mass-impairment as soldiers returned from the horrors of trench-warfare. The war was followed by creation of some rehabilitation schemes and villages but largely there was no 'land fit for heroes'.
1920s and 1930s	The medical, charitable and institutional approaches to disability continued to dominate on a national level. The increased interest in Eugenic theory in Europe and America culminated in the ideas of a pure and perfect race which were the foundation of Nazism.
1940s	The 2nd World War also created impairment and disability on a large scale, but this time the state response included the creation of the welfare state in 1948.
1950s	Various acts of legislation gave more support to disabled people in employment, education and welfare services. The foundation of carer-led charities in the UK was a departure from big institutions run by medical experts.
1960s	Disabled people, sometimes in partnership with carers, began to set up their own organisations around issues such as motoring, income and recreational activities.
Early 1970s	Development of the independent living movement firstly in US, then in UK and Europe.
Mid-late 70s	Formation of user led groups and the social model of disability.
1981	International Year of Disabled People kick-started a more visible movement of disabled people and campaign for civil rights legislation.
1995	Disability Discrimination Act 1995.
Late 1990s	Increase in direct action campaigns alongside disability equality awareness and lobbying by disabled people's groups led to more rapid social and environmental change.
2003	European Year of Disabled People.
2007-2017	The global financial crisis led to a decade of austerity cuts which have seriously impacted on the independence and rights of disabled people and disability organisations.

So I've looked back in time, to all manner of interesting trends and phenomenon. My basic premise is that there's always been Impairment in some form or another throughout History and even Pre-History!

It starts with fossil records. When archaeologists look at fossil records, for example those of Hunter/Gatherers, they were always injuring themselves in fights and hunting situations with wild animals; falling out of trees and a wide range of other things!

There was no medical care, so people lived with broken bones, for starters; all kinds of herbal remedies would evolve. Later, you find in Chinese Culture, Egyptian Culture – most of the cultures of the world began to develop through interventions of medical practices.

And certain types of impairment, like blind people, would be encouraged; they were seen as having particular skills; in Egyptian culture they were harp players; in Ancient Chinese Culture, blind people were masseurs. So disabled people began to have defined roles.

They held positions of respect in societies, rather than being seen as disadvantaged: impairment wasn't viewed as disability, because there was more of a continuum of health.

There was more disease and disability anyway, the further back in history that we go, so it was probably viewed as more commonplace. If you were able-bodied, you were probably more unusual than the majority!

The whole purge of witches in Medieval Times, which was right across Europe, was based upon women and mental health. These days we would say, 'Oh that person has a learning disability,' – in medieval times they'd say, 'They're bewitched!'

If a woman gave birth to a disabled child they'd take the child out and leave him or her in the woods! And the woman would have the Badge of Evil! It was the Child of the Devil. Today these sound like awful practices, but, having said that, there are still cultures that think that way.

As David has explained, at one time, people with cerebral palsy were always called Spastics. I don't know whether he's ever told you the story of the surgeon who was lecturing his medical students about David's condition, without using the 'S' word. His students were completely puzzled until David interrupted and spelt the situation out to them!

The surgeon commented: 'As you can see, Mr Barnsley is a very forthright person!'

The word 'spastic' is actually a medical term and physiotherapists still use the term, in that environment: they'll refer to a 'spastic limb', meaning a limb where the muscles are contracted. It's part of medical terminology.

I think the problem was, it became a derogatory playground term of abuse: 'A Spaz'. There is a case for ironic language. Not everyone 'gets' this, but it's a bit like an Irish person saying, 'Well I'm a thick Paddy!' Or a Gay person saying: 'I'm a Queer!' So you're using derogatory language of the past as a kind of ironic humour, to make the situation more acceptable.

I would personally discourage that kind of approach, because you'll get a larger proportion of people saying, 'Well according to him it's ok to say 'Spastics'.' So it becomes negative again: bullying and hate-crime et cetera.

But who am I to tell someone of David's generation what language he should use to describe himself?! I think that applies to the older generation generally, doesn't it? That people take language with them to the grave and then the next generation and the one after that won't use those terms. David's mother told him that she didn't know the exact cause of his disability, but he believes it was a combination of premature birth and forceps.

From the 1950s onwards, there were probably more babies born with cerebral palsy (the two joint causes being forceps and lack of oxygen) because they probably survived that; also Polio affected a lot of people, particularly the more uneducated.

If you move on to the next decade, 1960s onwards, that was the Thalidomide era and so on. So my Timeline traces all the different changes and compares them. Also, by the 1960s is that there were a lot of different organisations, which, for the very first time, were run by disabled people themselves. There were Disabled Drivers Clubs, for instance, for people who drove their blue Trikes, like David. So there were clubs that disabled people were forming themselves.

In the 1960s there was a big protest march, to Trafalgar Square and the Trike Protest in the Houses of Parliament, when they were thinking of banning trikes; David describes being a part of that. They were lobbying their MPs but they managed to delay the demise of Trikes for quite a few more years. It was when Jim Callaghan was Prime Minister that he went there, with Mary and John Fletcher.

The 1950s and 60s was a great period of change for everybody wasn't it? The disabled people had their own circle of changes going on, within that wider social circle. For example the old courthouses in Ladywood being pulled down; people being shipped out to the suburbs, so that would have affected disabled children as well.

Disabled children have become more fully integrated into mainstream schools, during the last decade. In 1995 the *Disability Discrimination Act* became law, but even that took about ten years to implement.

The general consensus amongst those contributing to this book seems to be that there's still a tremendous amount to be done to improve facilities for the disabled. I think we may have gone a step or two backwards, as well. When the Act came out it was described as a 'dog with no teeth', because there was no way of people enforcing the law.

Then the government founded the *Disability Rights Commission*, which pursued cases, under the Law. That happened in 2000: people could get their legal costs paid so there were an increasing number of cases being heard. High street stores were being prosecuted, libraries and all manner of things.

Eventually, in 2010, the *Equality Act* replaced the *Disability Discrimination Act*, the *Race Relations Act* and the *Equal Opportunities Act*. So all of those, each with its own Commissioning Body, were all pooled under the *Equality Act*. Extra things were added, like Gender, Sexuality and Pregnancy, Age and Faith. You might think that was a good thing, to expand it, but unfortunately the result for Disability Groups and some of the others, is that they've become forgotten again," Pete concludes.

The *Steps to Independence* film was made by Brian Filkin, who visited various places, trying to get money and sponsors, for Carlson House, for the *MSA – The Midland Spastic Association*, as it was then called.

Tina Hackett started working at the *MSA* in 1984, in a building next door. She explains:

"In late 1984 my daughter was about six months old. A friend of mine, who I knew from the School, and had worked alongside, had a little bit of input at the Centre," Tina explains. "She found out that they were looking for somebody to do a few hours a week, physio-wise, because it was so difficult for adults with cerebral palsy to get physio.

At the time it wasn't considered necessary for adults with cerebral palsy to have physio, because the condition was regarded as non-progressive. So the idea was to put in maximum input, whilst the children were little; get them up to 18 – the school leaving age, then move them into the Adult Services. They'd been taught exercises, daily living, so they didn't require specialised help after that. That was very much the thinking.

Rather than being financially-motivated, this approach probably resulted more from medical ignorance – a lack of experience in working closely with children and adults with cerebral palsy.

I'm certainly not alone, but those people like myself, who worked intensely with cerebral palsy children, watched intently as they grew up; watched what happened when they went through their growth spurts and their adolescence, and what happened to a person's body, when they had cerebral palsy: having these spasms; everything is intensified. So if you have another illness on top of it, the mechanism of the cerebral palsy (and that varies unbelievably); everybody is different, so it's a very individual thing, as to how many symptoms are purely individual. It's fascinating, but it's an extraordinary condition. I could talk your head off, because it's something that has always been very close to my heart.

But the General Medicine people didn't understand the effect of having cerebral palsy. If you have arthritis you have certain symptoms – that's fine; you have certain treatment or you just take pain killers. If you have cerebral palsy and *then* you have arthritis, the cerebral palsy affects arthritis because of the degree of the spasms (increase in muscle tone).

You might have arthritis of the knee, so that affects all of the muscles in that leg, but that means that the increase in muscle tone that anyone else would feel, for someone with cerebral palsy that is intensified.

It then gets to such a point that you get what's called 'Overflow': you may not have arthritis in your other leg, but you may well have an 'affect', because of the cerebral palsy. So it can transfer elsewhere – perhaps to an arm. You might present with osteoarthritis of your right knee, but actually, you've got problems with your left shoulder... because of the 'Back-up System'!

It's an *enormous* subject. Certainly, with the spasms and the muscle tone, what happens is that the brain controls stimuli in the body, but with cerebral palsy there's not cut-off – so it's just constant stimulus!

For the rest of us, we've got an un-damaged nervous system: our body will reach the point where the brain says, 'I'm shutting that off! We've got enough muscle power.' That's how we can make a judgement about whether we're picking up an eggshell; something hot, or something heavy. Someone with cerebral palsy has the same amount of nerve stimuli being sent down to his fingers, but you don't get that damping down. It all revolves around our Central Nervous System.

In children and young adults it probably wasn't a higher frequency than in the general population, but, as you got older, the increase in arthritis would get worse; also, whatever else you might find happening to you and we all talk about the 'Downward Slide'...

In David's case, he's 76 now, at the time of writing, so he must have had at least one or two of those complications. It's more about, whatever you have, from a cold to something more serious, everything, depending on the degree of the cerebral palsy, will have a lesser or greater effect on anything that's wrong with you – and that's the difficulty of trying to explain, when you go to an appointment, 'I've got this problem.' Everyone is different and you need to take into account that this person also has cerebral palsy; very often that doesn't happen.

I spent about 11 years at the *MSA*, but generally-speaking, I've gone off on a physio tangent! The vast majority of my friends who I qualified with went, as I did, into a General Hospital. I started off there: it's now the Children's Hospital. I wanted to work with children; most of my friends have worked for the Children's Hospital.

I ended up going to Carlson House School, which was certainly a 'one-off'. After that I went back into the Community, working for *West Birmingham Community Paediatrics*... at most of the schools in Birmingham.

Then I joined the *MSA*. I didn't actually know very much about cerebral palsy in adults, although I knew a great deal more about the condition in children.

So I rang the Physio Department at the QE Hospital, which is literally just next door – and it's where I trained. I explained that I was working with adults with CP at the *MSA* and could they give me any advice? They said, 'I'd ring your local hospital if I were you.' So although it was my local hospital that was a bit of a Dead End.

I did lots of courses, lots of different things, but found that it was very difficult to find any information about management of CP for adults. I subsequently decided to continue working at the *MSA*, adapting what I had done to help children, to my work with adults. I developed my own ways of working. Again, when you think, experience-wise, (and you could do that in those days) it showed me that it worked.

I developed various stretches to help relieve the discomfort of spasticity; many of the people I was working with had difficulty with spasticity building up. They would then come back to me and say, 'Oh that was absolutely brilliant!' It was hard work and an intensive session, but they'd say, 'Oh, it lasted for three days... I could move!'

Then the flats were built right next to the Centre, where the school had been, so again, I had the remit, that if there were people working there I could then offer help and advice.

Princess Anne opened it – it was one of the highlights of my whole working career! The fact that it went slightly awry didn't really matter, because Princess Anne was so wonderful.

I used to go to the Monday Night Youth Club. People from next door knew that I would be there, so they would come round for advice, or to have a stretch, because quite a lot of them were working people. Perhaps a bit of massage and exercise. They'd say, 'That will set me up for the week now,' or for the month – or what-have-you.

As David explained in previous chapters, there were originally three clubs: Mondays: *Pathfinders*, for 21+ people; *Adventurers*, on Wednesdays, for people with mental difficulties; *Helping Hand* – up to 21 years of age.

David was subsequently able to move from the school, on a Friday night, down to the hut in Vicarage Road, where the *Helping Hand Youth Club* was held. The hut was later extended, to accommodate the craft work that went on during the day.

I provided a broad range of help – not just physio – I suppose it was an emotional outlet really. The difficulty of going to a hospital appointment or going into work; not being able to explain: 'I can't do this very simple thing, because I have cerebral palsy, which is having an effect on my whole body.' So sometimes they'd just come to talk, or do a few little exercises or stretches.

But most important of all, I was a Listening Ear: just letting people talk about things. I'm a great believer that: 'a problem shared is a problem halved'; especially with someone who had an understanding of what was involved. Occasionally I'd visit them, if there was a particular problem.

I also helped with Occupational Therapy: I used to do a lot of advocacy with people in the homes or the flats, where they needed specialised equipment.

David and Maureen both had contact with the Centre. I used to visit them. After I left the *MSA* I'd occasionally go to their Monastery Drive home, if needed. I know Barbara Brand very well," Tina concludes. "We used to work together."

Chapter Nine
More Hair-Raising Moments

In 1992, Betty Boothroyd was elected the first woman speaker of the House of Commons; Neil Kinnock and Roy Hattersley resigned as leader and deputy leader of the Labour Party. The Education Act established OFSTED, responsible for four-yearly school inspections.

Whitney Houston's 'I Will Always Love You' became a hit; James Ivory's film, 'Howard's End' was released; Michael Palin's television series, 'Pole to Pole' and Jennifer Saunders' 'Absolutely Fabulous', were first broadcast.

Meanwhile, I continued to have Trike Trouble! In 1991/92 it was suggested to me that the vehicle should be given a special treatment underneath, so that it didn't rust. So I handed my Trike in; if you hadn't got your Trike you could have a reserve machine, from Ashley Repairs, Hay Road, Hay Mills.

The Metro, with an automatic gearbox, which was always suspect, released all its oil in my mother's garage…she was very happy about that! It was stuck in her garage. I somehow managed to get home and I had the Trike. They tried to repair the Metro again, but this time oil flooded in front of the bungalow and in front of two other bungalows, in Harborne Park Road.

There I was, with Swarfega, trying to clear the mess up – in case somebody slipped on it. On Saturday afternoons we generally went to Maureen's mother's: she would always wash her best clothes for her and give us some food. Afterwards I'd usually take *my* mother out. As I couldn't do that – and I was a bit 'hyped up', because Maureen and I had had words, I went to pick the washing up from her mother, in Robin Hood Lane.

Jane Hall explains: "Nine times out of ten, the Trike broke down… and there were no mobile phones. The AA and RAC weren't equipped to fix it. At the time I was there, Dave had a Trike and a car. He'd take himself off on a Sunday night to visit Joe, at *The Beeches*."

Jenny remarks: "When we went out in David's Volvo we'd have a guided tour of all his accidents! Very reassuring: 'I went into a bus there'; or 'A bus knocked me over there!' 'My Trike broke down here.' I said, 'Bloody hell Dave, it's like a guided tour!'"

At the age of 51, as I was going over the traffic lights in Moseley Village/ Salisbury Road, my vehicle suddenly turned right – into the side of a bus! Joe will tell you about this: on seeing the wreckage afterwards, he was amazed that I'd survived! I claimed that the rod for the front wheel had not been tightened up... it had just come apart... with the shaking; but nobody would admit that.

All the people on the single-decker bus served me for whiplash. The police came; I was cut free by the Fire Brigade, it was in the paper, apparently, because there was chaos in Moseley!

I went into hospital and started to go into spasm. I lay there – beginning to feel the spasm coming on – and the viciousness... I kept asking them to notify my wife. So there I lay, in the Birmingham Accident Hospital, (the 'Acky' it was called) next to *Davenports*, for quite a long time.

The pain was coming on, so they gave me some 'laughing gas' ... as though I was having a baby! My voice was getting louder and I was getting worried about nobody notifying my wife. My mother was supposed to be coming – and-all-the-rest.

As far as my family were concerned I'd disappeared from the face of the earth! The police notified my wife at seven in the evening, although the accident had happened at about 3pm.

Eventually, a Doctor Johnson, who, to-the-best of-my-knowledge, became well known for getting the Air Ambulance Service going, treated me by setting the leg, then I was taken to the ward. There was all this equipment around me. They said, "We'll wait to see if your leg swells. If it doesn't we'll put it in plaster."

This other chap came round, with all of his student doctors, and said, "Oh Mr Barnsley, we'll put a cast on, but after six weeks we'll cut it and you'll be able to bend your legs and you'll be up walking!"

My wheelchair was at the side of my bed, so I said, "That will be a bleedin' miracle – I couldn't walk *before* I broke my leg!" He walked away – and never spoke to me again!

I was in a pretty poor state and, with all my earlier experiences of life, I thought my life was over. I was very aggressive and upset, because I was worried about my mother – and my wife, Maureen. I eventually gave up: I wouldn't eat; I wouldn't do anything. It was the worst accident experience that I've ever had!

They kept telling me that if I wanted to go on the toilet I must use the 'Monkey Pole'. I told them that I couldn't use it, as I had a fixed hip. They were quite nasty.

Tina Hackett arranged that I could sit in my wheelchair, with my foot up, so I'd get out of bed and go. After a while, I couldn't stand any more, so I wanted to go back into bed. Well, if you went to the Nurses' Station they seemed to be far too busy to do anything... chatting the doctors up – allegedly!

The young nurses were doing most of the jobs, on the ward. If I wanted to go to the toilet I had to get at least three bottles, because it would take hours before they came.

There was a Nursing Sister in charge on the ward, but they were under great stress. On Saturday nights all the drunks came in, were put in a bed, sobered up next day; then out they went again, with a bottle of whiskey!

But I remained in a very poor state. They said that I had to wait for Hospital Social Services, to resolve the situation with Maureen. So I hadn't been to the toilet for a week; I wasn't eating – and all the rest of it.

Maureen happened to be going to a *Crossroads Attendance Scheme* at that time. It was their Christmas Party. She had a word with Anita, who she got on with quite well with. Anita arranged an *MS* Bus for me, so I signed myself out, and went home.

When I got home, the *Crossroads Care Attendance Scheme* ladies, of which we knew quite a few, decided that they would look after me, until such time as Social Services got their act together. I was in quite a lot of pain but they sat me up in my wheelchair and it turned out that I had broken my leg in two places. I thought that it would never heal because all I'd got was bone: my legs never grew.

I'd got an old-fashioned, ceramic bedpan, the one that slides under; they don't have them now of course, they have disposable ones. Maureen, bless her, helped me onto that and I went to the toilet for the first time in weeks, because I was more relaxed, Maureen was absolutely wonderful, although she'd got her own problems.

Although I had the accident in November 1992, the plaster didn't come off until the following February. Tina stayed with me when that happened, because I was afraid of going into spasm. Social Services and the Care Attendance Scheme came in to help Maureen look after me, throughout that period.

On the day that my plaster was removed Tina helped me. She didn't tell me I had to be re-plastered up, for a different kind of leg support, but I managed to survive the day! I have been eternally grateful to her for that. She stayed with me in hospital, while it was done.

Tina elaborates: "He had this accident and one leg was put in plaster. One of the things I'd learned from work that I'd done in the past, was that with cerebral palsy, if you're going to put one leg in plaster you had to do the same to the other leg. Otherwise, the tension would build up so much that you would then actually cause this awful imbalance – and the pain would be dreadful! It was extremely difficult.

"There was a particular technique of supporting the toes, because the traditional way of plastering somebody's foot is to leave the toes out. But if you have cerebral palsy and particularly if you have diplegia or quadriplegia if you don't have a support under your toes, what will happen with a spasm is that your toes will curve and then just go on curling; the spasm gets worse and goes up your leg, up into your thigh, into your hip – then down into the other leg. You'll be completely immobilised, disabled – and on your own – you can't do anything about that. Once that's happened, it's very difficult to stop it happening!

"So the technique that we used with children was to have the plaster going under the toes, just pushing them up slightly. Then on the front you'd still keep the toes exposed, so you could check the colour of them. But that then meant that you didn't induce a spasm, which would affect the whole of your body.

"Sometimes with the children, depending upon the severity of the spasm we would sometimes put the other foot in plaster, but one leg was enough with David.

"I got the call from David, that he was in such agony and such terrible trouble – and I believe he'd been asking them to contact me. They said, 'It's not necessary. We've got people here and we know what we're doing!'

"I went along and eventually managed to persuade them to re-do the cast and do it the way I wanted. Once we'd re-done it and I managed to stretch David's toes and relieve the spasm, you could just see it in his face. Even the chap who was doing the plastering said to me, 'I've never seen that done before.' I said, 'I've worked with children for many years. This is how we always do it.' He said, 'Look at him now – his face has changed.' I said, 'Yes, because he's no longer in pain.'

"For somebody like myself, who was doing it from experience and knew that it worked, it wasn't a big thing; but for David it made the world of difference.

"I also did a lot of hospital visits with Maureen," Tina continues. "One that stands out in my mind was when she had to have a shoulder X-Ray. David was waiting outside and I went in with her. The procedure is, they position you on the bed; we go behind the screen and then they say, 'One, two three – hold your breath!' I told the lady, even before we started, that I would have to assist Maureen. We had to put her up onto the bed, because there wasn't any other way of doing it. I said, 'Once Maureen is still, then don't say anything, because you'll startle her – and you'll lose her.'

"She startled very easily – and she'd go all over the place. It was very difficult to get her calm and I'd like to think that part of our success in doing that was because I was there – quietly talking to her. Talking to her all the time; she keeping still and then saying quietly that I had to leave her to go behind the screen – 'Just stay still and keep calm.' Then I'd go behind the screen and say to this lady, "Just do it!" This woman tried to do it her own way six times. Finally in

Maureen in happier days: she always enjoyed water... and Jacuzzis in particular, which 'tickled her fancy'. Taken at the Jane Hodge Hotel, near Cowbridge; a two-edged sword, because she swallowed much of the chlorine-treated water, which made her ill!

exasperation, we did it my way – and it worked! We used to do swimming classes from the *MSA* as well."

She also loved danger Tina – she married me, didn't she?!

"Maureen loved the water," Tina continues. "We used to go to *Cocksmoor Woods Leisure Centre* and we also had a contact with the *Martineau Centre* – the *Teacher's Centre*: the one that's been knocked down. It was the best one but it's a housing estate now. It had a lovely little pool, with good changing rooms and atmosphere.

"We had some very enjoyable times there. Maureen, God-bless-her, was a very outspoken lady," concludes Tina.

The upshot of the Moseley accident was that my mother was having an ischemic attack; they got my trike back to me very quickly, but meanwhile, I was having a lot of trouble with the Fire Brigade. The Fire Station was three hundred yards down on the left. If you were involved in any road accident you had to notify them immediately, but you weren't to get involved in any negotiations.

The Fire Brigade wanted me to pay for their assistance. But the vehicle was on loan to me – it belonged to the *Wheel Chair Service*, which was in Selly Oak – near the *Acorns Hospice*: the *Artificial Limb and Appliance Centre*.

Although the Brigade kept writing to me, while I was lying in bed. I continued to refer them to the *Wheelchair Centre.*

To add insult to injury, the *Invalid Vehicle Service* wrote to us saying that the Trikes would be maintained for the foreseeable future... the next two years. I wrote back to point out that they'd been using old parts!

Regarding the passengers who were suing me for Whiplash, someone from the Insurance Company came to see me and I explained what had happened. Although they said that they would look into it, they just left it.

I got my spare vehicle back, although it was about six months before I could use it. Then I had to do a Police Statement, which I signed.

Do you think the *Invalid Vehicle Service* would admit liability?! Their headquarters were in Blackpool by the way.

At one point, the police were going to charge me. Luckily, I happened to have the advice of a solicitor, from *Sydney Mitchell.* He said, "David, they're going to charge you with careless driving. Keep your mouth shut and pay the fine, otherwise they will charge you with much more." That just showed me how ineffectual the police system was. So that's what I did.

Eventually, when Maureen got the Independent Living Allowance Jane Hall left *Goldsborough* and Maureen employed her on that basis... she became a very firm friend. She saw Maureen and me through a few scrapes – and what-have-you, right up until Maureen's death.

Her Independent Living Allowance stopped when she died and she left money to the Stables, where she used to go riding.

As things became worse, Maureen became more dependent upon the drink. Eating was always a problem as well. She always carried a man's handkerchief, to mop her mouth. She drank; she smoked and if she'd have had the chance she'd have gone out with men as well. But she had a life of sorts.

But we have to see it from her viewpoint. Because she'd been like that from birth, hadn't she? It must have been so frustrating for her. Even as a child, she was talking about suicide. And two able-bodied people in her family *did* commit suicide: allegedly, they drank themselves to death.

Meanwhile, Maureen was getting on a bit. She was begging people to give her tablets. She drank every night; fell on the floor. I'd be listening to her – struggling to get back into bed... about 2 o'clock in the morning. It was a nightmare!

"Then I had a phone call in 2000," Jenny recalls. "David just simply said, 'Maureen's dead!'

"I said, 'Oh dear Dave. What happened?' He explained that she'd gone to the toilet in the early hours and must have keeled over, on to the wheelchair. Her face landed in the cushion. She didn't have the physical strength to lift her face. The police came round and there was an Inquest: the verdict was Asphyxiation."

The funeral was held at Robin Hood Cemetery. In Hall Green, Birmingham.

In the Crematorium grounds, one of the guests reached out to stop someone falling – but it pulled her over as well. Unbeknown to me, who had other things on my mind, there was a yellow ambulance outside, which carted her off to hospital! Joe was in hospital at the time, so he couldn't attend.

But the chapel was absolutely packed. I knew all of Maureen's friends and relatives. They were standing up at the back. My two Mustin aunts were sitting elsewhere. I suddenly had a strong feeling within me… that I needed to be near them – so I went over and sat with them.

For the Wake, we went back to Monastery Drive. Jane and I decided that we would have the buffet there. Relatives of Maureen's attended the funeral, including some from Wales. They were under the impression that Maureen had fallen over, hit her head and died! In fact she'd fallen off the toilet!

But at least the weather kept fine for us.

Jenny recalls: "I went to Maureen's funeral – and then back to Monastery Drive afterwards. The bungalow was packed. Unfortunately, I had to leave early, to pick Amy up from school, so I wasn't there to the 'bitter end'. But yes – people were spilling out into the garden.

"Maureen was well loved: she was a lovable rogue; she had a lot of Carers at that time; you could not *help* but be fond of her. You'd just want to help her. There was absolutely nothing wrong with her brain: it was getting her body to do what her brain wanted to do. She couldn't pronounce 't 'e.g. 'kekkle'. Her tongue was trapped behind her teeth: that was the worst problem for her. She would say something – and I would try and understand what she said; there'd be this awful pause, when I was trying to work out what it could have been. Then she'd say it again."

Jane Hall explains: "After Maureen died in 2000 David was still driving, but it reached the stage where he decided to give it up. He'd been talking about it for a while. So I started to drive for him, in the old vehicle, which was a bit more difficult. It was a much heavier vehicle. We'd go out for coffee, to Beckett's Farm; shopping; Solihull."

Jenny remembers, "I returned, after Maureen's death, for a week or two, then continued helping him, for three days a week. I became ill, between 2009 – 2010, then I returned for one day a week, to start with, because I still felt quite weak; I did that for a while, but gradually increased to two days a week, while other people filled in the gaps."

Still on the subject of 'Hair-raising Moments', but moving on a few years, I planned to have Christmas Lunch with a friend at *Chateau Impney*, in 2012. Jenny was with me when I paid them a preliminary visit.

"When Dave wasn't very au fait with a place he used to reconnoiter it first, a day or two ahead. He needed to know where he could park, how many steps; can

I get to the table? Even a table with a chair leg in the way would make a huge difference; the height – everything," explains Jenny.

On 1st October, just a few weeks before that Christmas Lunch, a new Government Act had come into force, that all public places should have Disability Access. The entrance to *Chateau Impney* therefore had a new 'Disabled Access' sign at the entrance.

"So we went out to Lunch there beforehand, to sort it out, because you didn't want that performance on Christmas Day, with things not working out!" Jenny continues.

"We went in, and the manager greeted us saying, 'Oh yes, you'll be in the restaurant downstairs, for your Christmas Lunch.' So David asked to go down there, because if he couldn't get down there that day, he wouldn't be able to do so for his Christmas Lunch. The manager said, 'Yes sir – we've just had this lift installed, so it will be able to take you down.' There was also a curved white rail attached to it, leading down there.

"The lift wasn't enclosed: it was like a motorized platform, attached to the wall. It had edges, but not a roof. Dave said, 'I don't think I'll be able to get in that, off my wheelchair – and I'm a heavy weight myself.'

'No problem sir, it takes a weight of 250 kilos.' But Dave said, 'I don't think it will hold me!' He said, 'It will sir!'

"So David got into it," Jenny continues, "and I suppose, because of gravity, it did start to go down. But then half-way down, possibly because of the curve, it stopped … And it wouldn't go down and it wouldn't go up! As on a Ferris Wheel, there was a bar in front of David… he was hanging on to that. But he was hanging, almost in mid-air, on to this rail – not being able to go anywhere. He was quite good humoured about it, because normally, in any situation like that, he panics… and gets a bit aggressive. But he was laughing: 'How am I going to get out?!'

"Anyway, the manager came and said, 'Don't worry sir, we'll get it sorted.'

"His staff were mainly Polish, so they didn't understand much English. They were trying to lift him out, but David said, 'No, you need to send for the Fire Brigade.' The manager said that wouldn't be necessary and that the lift manufacturers were in Leicester. So there was a back-and-forth conversation between Dave and the manager, with Dave asking him to fetch the Fire Brigade and the manager repeating over and over that there was no need for that.

"Eventually David said, 'And what's your name?' Because this was taking *forever*. I was at the bottom of the staircase, looking up… absolutely in hysterics! I was laughing so loud that people coming out of the restaurant were coming over too: 'Come and have a look at this!' They were using the pretext of going to the toilet, so that they could see what was happening.

"When the manager told David that his name was Robin, Dave said, 'Oh – my name's Batman… Fly off and get the Fire Brigade!'

"Although he's normally aggressive when he panics, Dave was being quite funny," Jenny continues. "So in the end, Robin had to ring the Fire Brigade. All these firemen came in – which was very nice! They had to get the wheelchair in place so that he could be lifted out, but as soon as they did that, the lift shot up – to the top of the stairs! Like the air going out of a balloon. However, they'd put him in his wheelchair by then; the whole incident lasted around an hour.

"It was one of those situations when you had to *be* there. They finally got him upstairs, by carrying him up there in the wheelchair; they must have been so strong. The manager said, 'I can't apologise enough.'

"Had it been a manual wheelchair it would have been fine, but these electric wheelchairs weigh tons. The manager offered him a meal but Dave said, 'Forget it – I'm too upset. And I'm not coming on Christmas Day.' The manager rushed out to us with this *Chateau Impney* rose bowl.

"We sat in the car, but then he had a delayed reaction, so we waited for a while, then David drove us back," Jenny concludes.

Chapter Ten

Oxygen to the Rescue – and Mon Ami Mate

I had a 60th Birthday Party at the Ramada, in Solihull, in 2001, but unfortunately, the hotel didn't display the table plan on the wall, or provide the food I'd ordered – including a birthday cake with a picture of a car on it. I'm very keen on cars; not so much on motor-racing now, but I used to go to Silverstone. My 70th and 75th parties were far happier occasions.

David Barnsley

There was wheelchair incident at the Queen Elizabeth Hospital. Understandably, my past history with hospitals, has given me an aversion to them, (including my 'Guinea Pig' treatment and so on).

My friend, Jenny Willock, effectively saved my life. I went with her to Moseley Hall Hospital in 2011. I now know that they've got a standard procedure. If your health worsens they ask you if you want to be resuscitated. I'd previously said no. I had further breathing difficulties and I was 'sinking', so they took me to the Queen Elizabeth Hospital in Birmingham. Jenny was with me again and they said to her, 'He doesn't want to be resuscitated,' because it was on my medical records.

Jenny asked them to keep me alive, so they gave me an extra hour. Luckily I recovered, but it was her fast-talking that saved me!

I've since rescinded that instruction with my doctor, so that it doesn't happen again. Jenny's listed as my 'next-of-kin', so they would automatically notify her. But in this case, luckily, she was with me.

"They don't know how to handle him," Jenny explains. "He's got this 'Charnley Hip', which is completely fixed; it's named after Mr Charnley, the Consultant who originally treated him, at Hume Hospital, Manchester. He was later knighted for his pioneering work. Dave used to go into spasm and his hip would jump out," continues Jenny. "But young doctors and nurses don't understand the history of it. Mr Charnley fixed it so he can't bend it – that's why it's in that position.

"So when Dave was in hospital and particularly when he was in the QE, because he wasn't compos mentis, he was in a Triage Ward; by the time I reached him, they'd already put him in a bed.

"Any of the medics who came to see him, naturally wanted to straighten his leg. I was constantly saying, 'Don't touch his leg; don't try to straighten it; don't put your arm under his knees, to maneuver him.' I said, 'Put it on his notes – put a sign above his bed. 'Do not touch my leg'. They said, 'Oh no, we can't do that, for confidentiality reasons!' I protested: 'You could break his hip!!'

"So every nurse that came, immediately went to his legs. I repeated: 'Don't touch his legs!' Honestly, I was like a dripping tap! I made them write a big label over his notes: 'Don't touch the legs'."

Jenny's husband, Pete, then had to somehow transport Dave's electric wheelchair, to the Queen Elizabeth!

"That was when Dave was suddenly taken into the Intensive Care Unit," Pete recalls. "Jen rang me about three o'clock in the morning. Immediately, the next day, to get him out of bed, they had to put him in a wheelchair. I got his wheelchair and put it into his truck. When we reached the QE I got it out again, but the only way I could get it uphill was astride of it. I'd never been in one before. It has a Giro-stick, so I drove it all the way up and into the hospital, learning as I went along.

"As we reached the lifts, I backed it in, went into the ward and asked them where to park it! I parked it in a corner, heaving a huge sigh of relief!" Pete continues. "You're talking about £14,000 worth of equipment. I told the person on the ward desk, 'They're going to think I'm a Miracle Patient, because I've just come in by wheelchair – and I'm walking out!'"

"It must have been about one o'clock in the morning, when they got round to seeing him," Jenny continues. "They gave him something to make him comfortable and I kept saying, 'What's going to happen?' 'What are you going to do?' I eventually got the doctor, just after 1am by which time my daughter had come to join me... She was worried.

"They asked me what Dave's quality of life was like. I said, 'Well, he's all right. He goes out and about,' and I explained about the care that was available where he was living. They explained that the decision they were about to make all depended upon his quality of life. I was totally shocked.

"They decided to put him on oxygen for an hour – to see what happened. If there was any improvement they would discuss it again. My daughter, Amy and I were shoved into a side room for an hour, in Intensive Care. It was really upsetting," (begins to cry).

"Anyway, after an hour we were allowed to go and see him. And he was a new man. It was the oxygen, coursing through his lungs that saved him. It's difficult for him to get rid of the carbon dioxide in his lungs. But the oxygen pushes that out: that's why he's on oxygen at night – now.

"He had a portable tank on his wheelchair, but that didn't work out... the tube was strangling him! He's on oxygen for eight hours, every night. Which is why, when he says that he's going to die, I say, 'What are you going to die of?! You're probably going to die of laughing!'

"When he went back into Intensive Care it was miraculous! At the time it was just a case of I couldn't say, 'Don't bother!' I wouldn't take the credit unnecessarily."

But the thing is, if Jenny hadn't been there, it could have been an entirely different story, because according to my notes I'd previously asked not to be revived... they would have found the DNR, which went before. But when I'm not well or have to go into hospital, I need someone with me. I think Jane Hall was on holiday.

As you'll see from one of the opening pages, this book is dedicated to my *lifelong* friend, Anthony Sutton, BA (Hons) and MBE. He had a particular gift for languages, especially Russian and Spanish. We refer to him in other chapters too. He died quite recently, on 8 November 2012.

Photo taken on 5 March 1995, on the front drive of Anthony and Joan Sutton's home, The Stables, Knifton, near Ashbourne, Derbyshire. Anthony's white Subaru is in the background. David and Maureen are in the front seats of their Honda Accord Estate, it was hand-controlled. Raj used to help load wheelchairs into the back of that car, in which they enjoyed many National Trust excursions.

David and Anthony in Porthcawl. They travelled there in separate vehicles, staying at the Jane Hodge Hotel.

Roger Robinson comments: "Anthony couldn't walk, but he was very good at translating – that was his main job. I think he worked freelance. He was a very sociable chap: we all got on very well together. He did very well getting a degree under those circumstances."

It's amazing that my friend excelled at languages, despite his speech difficulties.

I've spent my whole life, from 1959 – 2011, driving to a cornucopia of interesting places. Up until recently, Pete would drive me out to various places of interest.

One of our more recent trips to Meriden, was hardly memorable...it poured down with rain! I can't afford to go out for long days now, so Pete suggested Meriden, as it's a short drive. I don't eat out any more, whereas years before, I used to go to the Cotswolds, on a weekly basis. My fridge magnets, show the range of places I've visited.

Going to Meriden revived memories for me, because I used to go to Torrington Avenue there; a convertor, Jim Duran, adapted my car's hand controls. But this time the heavens opened, so I was trapped in my car. Pete went to the café for a cup of coffee. I drank that in the car and then we came home! But at least it was out of here – four walls! Pete recalls some of our other trips:

"I went over to the Black Country with him, Jubilee Autos, in Wednesbury, to get his new vehicle. In these special vehicles, they have a lower floor – they cut the petrol tank down. On one unfortunate occasion we'd been out for a ride in Worcestershire and were coming back. We'd got as far as Kings Norton Green, a couple of miles from home, when it ran out of petrol, although the gauge said over a quarter full. When they modify these things they don't modify the petrol gauge.

"Dave panicked: 'We're going to be stuck here all night!' We were on Parson's Hill and cut out just before the canal bridge. I rang Jen straight away and she came out with some petrol. The AA man told me afterwards that it wouldn't start because it was leaning backwards.

"An AA man towed us back. Dave told everybody about it afterwards: that he was in danger – and how he thought he was going to be there all night! He always thinks the worst if things go wrong, whereas I try to ignore it and take the more optimistic view.

"He sometimes doesn't know what to do or where to go, but he's determined to go out: he's not going to just sit in that place all day, every day! What I try to do is surprise him. He'll say that he'd like to go out for a drive, but then I'll take him to somewhere like Barr Beacon, where he hasn't been for twenty-five years; then I took him to the Clent Hills; the part that belongs to *English Heritage* – we had a cup of tea there. I took him to *Packwood House* and he's always shocked: 'You won't be able to get in.' I said, 'It's all been done; it was rebuilt two years ago'."

One of the aspects we examine in this book are improvements for the Disabled, over the years. Despite improved access in some establishments many public buildings remain un-adapted.

"We'd visited Kidderminster, one winter, three years ago, then went on to Bridgnorth," Pete continues. "We didn't take the train – we drove there. We were in a Square in Bridgnorth and were going to have Lunch at one of the pubs, but it hadn't got a ramp. I ended up going into a Fast Food Store, to buy sandwiches! So that's the kind of situation that Dave's talking about.

"It depends on the organisation that you're going into. Now we've been on a train a few times – the *Severn Valley Railway* – and it's all arranged. There's a certain carriage, with a Guard, who puts the ramps out; sees you in. They look after you, because they've got dedicated carriages for it. So there *are* some good things."

"We had to go to Leamington, to pick up some curtains from the Retail Park," interjects Jenny. "Dave said, 'We'll have some lunch while we're here.' We went to a pub, just outside the Retail Park, but we couldn't get in, because there were wooden steps. Dave has to eat, because he goes a bit funny if he doesn't... a sandwich is never an option. So I went in the pub and explained the situation; they felt quite badly about it. We sat back in the truck and the pub management sent waiter service out to us, with hot food! It was quite amusing – but all credit to them!"

"In the summer, we'd regularly go to the Cotswolds. We used to go to a pub called the *Howard Arms* at Illmington. But then the ownership changed, it was open all day, and the image changed... and David hated it," Pete remembers.

"It had been a place where everyone knew each other; very friendly – with the personal touch: 'Oh hello Mr Barnsley!' But it lost that atmosphere when it became an all-day pub. But the owner's sons moved on to a place called the *Horse & Groom*, at Bourton-on-the-Hill, just above Moreton-in-Marsh. So we started to go there regularly and it was personal service again: 'Hello Dave!' They'd reserve a table for us. Unfortunately they've just sold that and it's not going to be the same. So we've not been in since.

"I'm very much into World War I History, so things like Commonwealth War Graves, when I spot them, I take Dave back to see them," Pete continues. "There was one in Moreton-in-Marsh and his friend, Anthony, actually worked at the *Fire Training College*, when he was in the Government. He won the MBE for 30 years of sterling service there, as a civil servant.

"The old aerodrome is where they taught people to fly Wellington Bombers. A lot of the graves, in the Commonwealth War Grave Cemetery are of people who have crashed, on take-off and landing. So they aren't war casualties as such, but those who were learning to operate during the war.

"At the bottom of Bourton-on-the-Hill is a caravan park and opposite it is a private museum of Wellington Bombers. It's only open on Sundays, so David asked me if I'd take him on a Sunday.

"He's very interested in History, although he doesn't like war," Pete observes. "Another time, I took him to Snitterfield, which was another bomber base and the museum there, which goes back to the Middle Ages, with knights-in-armour and so on. There are a lot of collections in there, which have been loaned.

"So Jenny helps Dave twice a week and I take him out once a week. If I take him out on Saturdays it's usually the Hippodrome matinee – he loves that! I've taken him to the Solihull Arts Centre to plays and musicals. The last one we went to was Joe Brown, without the 'Bruvvers'. Previous to that we went to see the *Glen Miller Story* – that was good; I've taken him to quite a few," Pete concludes.

Chapter Eleven

Empowering People

In 1947, Britain faced economic crises, caused by the resumption of convertibility of the pound – and the particularly severe winter that year (lakes, rivers and canals froze over!)

In that same year, the coal industry was nationalized... and the school-leaving age raised to 15.

The musicals 'Brigadoon' and 'Finian's Rainbow' were first performed and the soon-to-be iconic 'Diary of Anne Frank' was published. Tennessee Williams' new play 'A Streetcar Named Desire' had a huge impact on theatre audiences.

Prime Minister Clement Attlee made the BBC's first UK Party Political Broadcast. It also marked the death of an equally famous political figure, Stanley Baldwin, aged 80, in March of that year.

That same year, *Cerebral Palsy Midlands* (*CPM*, formerly the *MSA*) embarked on its vital mission, to empower disabled people.

Shirley interviewed two highly experienced members of their ranks: Community Social Worker Barbara Brand and Gary Watson, Manager at *Cerebral Palsy Midlands*, provide an overview of its history, comparing and contrasting David's life with that of other disabled people.

"I became manager in 2012. Before that I was the Assistant Manager, following my initial job as Day Centre Officer. I first started working here in 1999," recalls Gary.

Barbara Brand explains, "I started here in November of 1981, as a Welfare Officer. David Barnsley and I first met when he was a Trustee for the *Midlands Spastics Association*, in the mid-1980s; he was on our Council. I met his wife, Maureen, later on when I did Day Visits. At that time, Maureen and David lived in a bungalow, in Harborne Park Road."

Gary's first association, in respect of David and Maureen, was when he was charged with the job of taking a group from the *Midlands Spastics' Association* as it used to be called, to Maureen's funeral.

"It's quite a funny story – although it wasn't funny at the time! I took a group of disabled people from our organisation, to the *Beeches*, to pick up the funeral, which would be a hearse and quite a convoy of traffic. I got flashed to actually lead the convoy, so I was the first person behind the hearse," Gary explains.

"We were going to the *Robin Hood Cemetery* in Hall Green, Birmingham; it was a burial. But I lost the hearse – I must have had twenty to thirty vehicles behind me – and did not know where I was going!

"So, at the time, it was the worst thing that could have happened to me, because it was my responsibility. The convoy split up and we ended up all getting to the ceremony slightly late. I don't think David was aware of this. As he explained in Chapter 9, one of our people fell over.

"So that was my first association with the Barnsleys. I met David officially about a year later, at one of our social clubs, because he was a Committee Member. He was very outspoken and a strong character – that's why he sticks in my mind. He would have been available for a General Meeting of the Association of the *MSA*, because it was held on the same night as the *Pathfinders Social Club*, although I understand that David never actually joined that *particular* club, having met Maureen by that time.

"Part of my job was to organise and support that club, which was founded in the 1950s. Its title was a reference to World War II."

Barbara describes Maureen, as a very intelligent lady: "She had a lot of physical challenges, which I think she found difficult to come to terms with. But she never lost her femininity: she liked to dress very stylishly; she used to like to wear jewellery; always had perfume on.

"I think she struggled with the fact that her sister was quite a glamorous lady – that probably impacted upon Maureen.

"She had a lot of high standards, which she always maintained – and so did David: they both had very high standards. I used to enjoy visiting them. Maureen would talk to me, woman-to-woman, sometimes.

"Although she was difficult to understand," Barbara continues, "working with people who have speech impairment, made it easier for me than someone who didn't. So communication between the two of us was good.

"That was one of the challenges for Maureen, because when she was outside, with the general public, she couldn't make herself understood. Often, she had to have someone talking for her – and that made it seem as though she had quite a bit of learning difficulty – which she most certainly did not.

"We talked quite a bit about clothes: what I was wearing; perfume et cetera. Things that she couldn't really talk to David about, as they were feminine subjects. She didn't talk much about intimate struggles; some days she would be down more than others – so then she'd mention what might be bothering her. But usually, it wasn't conversation at an in-depth level. Maureen's condition, as you've already learned, was Athetosis: (she was an Athetoid).

"My relationship with Maureen was different to the one I had with David, who tends to 'bare his soul' more. He will say things as they are, whereas someone else might be more politically correct, in some ways. In my opinion, although David comes out as rather a brash person, I know him very well, and he's really quite kind-hearted," observes Barbara.

At least one of our other contributors to this book has suggested that David likes to be the centre of attention, because of his early upbringing, but, in fact, David considers himself to be the direct opposite: "I'm naturally more inclined to hold back. Although my surface reaction to situations resembles someone who needs to feel in control, inside I'm quite a 'softie'!"

"I do know that he's a very sensitive person," agrees Barbara. "He will say things and then reflect on them – and worry about them: he is a worrier; he will be concerned about whether he has said the right thing. But that may not come across to people: they *may* think he's outspoken.

"I had to do two visits per year, to people who were on our register," she continues, "whether they wanted me to or not! Sometimes I had to put my card through the door. Other times I would visit, because there was a genuine problem that they couldn't deal with themselves. So they would call upon me, to try to help them sort it out.

"If I went on a routine visit and there wasn't anything specific, then I would just talk to them about things in general. The Barnsley home was always immaculate; it's still the same today. They enjoyed their time in Harborne Park Road. It had quite an impact upon David, when they moved to Monastery Drive, because it was actually owned by Maureen's family and David felt as if he was in their debt.

"He was no longer in charge of his residential circumstances – he didn't like that at all. Although the bungalow was quite small, it met their needs, but Monastery Drive was palatial; it was a beautiful house, but it wasn't what he perceived as his domain."

How have facilities for the disabled improved, over the years?

"Well the facilities have definitely *improved*; whether they are *sufficient* is another question," observes Gary. "I don't think there's enough consultation with disabled people about this: maybe the people who are looking at accessibility facilities for the disabled don't necessarily have all the relevant information, although the intention for improvement is there. As an example we can just take our transport systems, such as buses. You can have the facilities, but if the driver isn't trained, it's really a waste. It's the same with taxis; *Ring-and-Ride* availability."

When they first installed automatic doors on buses. Maureen was used to the old system, so she got caught in the new doors: the bus started dragging her along – a really dangerous situation!

"And she wouldn't have been the only one Shirley! When you look at the new Birmingham City Centre buildings that are being created, it's still not very accessible, if you're actually in a wheelchair... and these are modern buildings," Gary continues.

"So, they have improved... but not all disabled people can access these facilities; especially if they've got speech or communication problems.

"Lifts can be a problem too, although mostly they're now built to a reasonable size. I can tell you a story about being with a disabled group from Wolverhampton, on the Metro Line. It's a fantastic service: it runs from Snow Hill to Wolverhampton.

"We were doing Travel Training: trying to get people to use the local facilities... to support this, as best we can. There were two problems with the Metro Line: when we were travelled to Snow Hill Station the lifts weren't working. We reached the platform, but we couldn't access Birmingham. So we had to get back on the Metro, to go back to the station; this isn't unusual, especially when you're working.

"Probably the biggest thing about that trip, was that, in Wolverhampton, we were a group of seven or eight people, with half of us being disabled – and even though the Metro was there, we couldn't actually get our group on, because with the amount of people waiting for it, it filled up very quickly. Although we were waiting there, forming an orderly queue, we had to wait for the next ...and the driver had to stop the general public from getting on!

"We didn't phone in advance, because normally it's accessible for wheelchairs, from the platform, but if the general public won't let you on, because they're just rushing to get home themselves..."

Jane Hall was saying that if there's one thing that most needs improving in relation to disability, it's re-educating the public.

"Which is the point I'm making," Gary continues. "As an able-bodied person, I've witnessed time and time again, that you can have the facility, but generally, we tend to live in a society which is less caring – and if you're not only physically disabled, but also have communication difficulties, people's perception of you can vary so much."

"One of the saddest things I can say: I started back in 1981 – and however much money has been ploughed into improving the lives of disabled people; whether it be with infrastructure or attitude, there seem to be a lot *less* disabled people accessing the community," observes Barbara. "It's people's attitudes. I think we are very image-led today, especially young people. Adult Disability is not very image-based; that's one of the factors," she continues.

"David was fortunate, in having the opportunity of a school of selection – and he was given that confidence of mind, which took you and your fellow pupils on, for when you were older.

"He was actually one of the success stories of Carlson House School, where pupils were selected as young children and they were nurtured; they were given a lot of self-confidence, by going through that process. They were expected to achieve and therefore they *did* achieve. That's possibly one of the main differences between that school and others.

"The staff-pupil ratios were also very good there – that was very important. Probably the *Institute for Conductive Education* in Moseley, covered a similar course, but that stopped at the age of eleven or twelve. That's on Cannon Hill Park. It's still there – just at the side of the *MAC Centre*.

"Another of our concerns is the integration, or otherwise, of disabled children into mainstream schooling. There seem to be different schools of thought on this. As a former schoolteacher of 25 years' experience, I'm inclined to think that Special Schools would, generally-speaking, be better for disabled children, as they'd get more relevant teaching time.

"A Primary School teacher, would normally teach approximately ten different subjects to 30 pupils, so everyone is going to suffer if you then introduce disabled pupils into the situation.

"Carlson House School was closed shortly after the Warnock Report, but I believe that around 2005, Lady Warnock published a pamphlet, saying that she had changed her mind."

"To my knowledge the Warnock Report was about how children's education can be best served," Gary comments. "It was decided that children would develop better and more normally in society, if that's the right word, by going through the main education system. But I don't think it was clear enough, in the sense that it's not suitable for all.

"However, it has to be a positive thing, for an individual with a disability – that they can access mainstream education on an equal basis – for certain people," he continues.

"Disability can affect people on so many levels. When we quote the figure that 1 in 4 babies may have some disability, there's going to be a high proportion of those people who can be integrated into society, living independent, productive lives.

"I think David would still have been quite independent, if he'd had a mainstream education. Your physical disability would have held you back, but you have led a successful life."

One of our other contributors said something very similar, Gary – that David was a perfect example of someone who would have benefitted from modern mainstream schooling. But the problem was that once he'd started working for

Lucas's (which he did for twenty-five years) he just couldn't keep up in the workplace.

So, if someone like David was put into a mainstream school now, his problem would be lack of speed. He simply would *not* be able to keep up with what the able-bodied pupils were doing.

Gary argues: "If you're actually identified as having a Special Need, so you're put into a Special Environment, which some people do need, you'll develop within that environment.

"We can't do a lot for some of the people who are in the 30-50 age bracket now, but if you do get a child who is young enough, or as a baby, they can go to mainstream schools and we can identify their needs at primary school level.

"However, we're in a very fast-paced society," he continues "and that can be very stressful and tough."

Barbara interjects: "Gary and I are very like-minded on so many things – I feel that if the provision is put into mainstream schools that *should* be put in, such as physiotherapy being actually on site and not visiting; also speech and language therapy on site, there is more chance of success.

"Also, society's 'take' on Disability is an important factor: whether that be with the teachers (some of the teachers are under so much pressure to perform and get exam results) that they could (I'm not saying that they do) feel that a disabled child would be something of an encumbrance.

"Furthermore, there is the mindset of certain children to be considered: bullying and name calling, can have a dramatic effect upon the growing child and the way in which they develop.

"So my consensus would be Special Schools are preferable – but I take Gary's point, that we don't live in a special world and when they finish school they've got to go out into the mainstream world.

"This is anecdotal, but a few years ago, I was tutoring a boy who has cerebral palsy, including speech difficulties – and a range of other obstacles to overcome. His mother is very intelligent and assertive, but even she has had an ongoing battle, trying to get sufficient help for her son, within the mainstream system. That's just one case that I know about from personal experience, but I shouldn't imagine that I'm on my own, in that respect."

"That case is not unusual," confirms Gary. "The people who tend to do better are those with strong family support. But there are so many families within our local area that are so isolated. They haven't got a voice and they're under the radar. They just get lost in the system, especially when they come out of education."

The mother I am referring to recently updated me, in the following two paragraphs, about the current situation regarding her son's education. He is now sixteen years old:

"In my experience, the problems intensify, when a disabled child moves from Junior to Senior School. As a child with difficulties gets older, the gap between himself and his able-bodied peers widens. It's almost like you're heading towards a dark tunnel, which becomes even darker as your child's needs increase.

"So the support for the individual and his family should be greater, at that stage. Unfortunately, it has been my experience that support significantly *decreases*, particularly in the case of schools that have become Academies – and are therefore self-funding."

"We try to access as many people as we can," Gary continues, "but there are people who we tend to pick up when they reach crisis point. So the people who have a strong support network, which says, 'No – I'm not going to stand for this,' are able to cope best, although the mother's predicament described above, would argue against that.

"However, it's all relative: there are a large proportion of disabled people who are completely under the radar and out of sight."

Our aim, within the confines of this book, is to produce a balanced picture of the situation, so we don't want to present too gloomy a picture; but at the same time it has to be realistic. Would you describe what the function of the *CPM* actually is?

"We are a Day Service for adults," explains Barbara "We *do* have an Advice and Advocacy Service, which crosses all ages. Gary can tell you more about the day-to-day running of the actual Centre. My job is to intervene when there's a need for Benefit advice; financial advice. Much of the bureaucratic system is very complicated, so many of our service users and their families can't really make their pathway through that. There have been so many changes, especially of late, that we will support and carry out what is necessary.

"As a typical situation, we've got a person with cerebral palsy, who is able to hold a tenancy, but is perhaps not very literate," she explains. "He is bombarded with lots of forms, so he will need a third person to help him manage his affairs, in whatever form that may take.

"What we try to do with people who are in the immediate vicinity is to ask them to bring round their correspondence – and I will see what needs to be done; we'll do it for them, on their behalf. So that's an immediate intervention of Advocacy," Barbara continues.

"We also supply a lot of emotional support, both to the individual themselves and to their families. We are instrumental in helping families who can no longer look after their disabled son or daughter with cerebral palsy, if they wish to move out. We try to do what's best for the whole family."

Do you refer to the people you help as 'clients', Gary?

"It's a grey area. Many years ago, Birmingham City Council brought in the term 'Service User'. That seems to be the key term, because we are all service users. But when you use that term, to connect to a disabled person, it depends upon what level you're working at. They can be referred by GPs, Social Services, and Families: all sorts of contacts.

"People who use our service are sometimes quiet; they are often known as 'attenders', because they are attending the service; that's also become a key word, over the years.

"Our catchment area covers all of Birmingham – and reaching into the Black Country. So the term 'client' is a grey area – because it seems so unconnected," he explains.

"We call the users of our service whatever they feel is appropriate, which is a bit of a difficult one, because they've all got different ideas," explains Barbara. "What we have done more of lately is to support people at the end of their lives. Many people living with CP or disability tend to be quite singular people; they haven't got the support of a partner.

"It can be a lonely existence. We have been involved with a few people, of late, who've reached the end of life and need quite a lot of support. That has been one of the most valuable things that we've branched out into," she continues.

Gary elaborates: "In the most recent cases it's about late 60s/early 70s. It just seems that in the last couple of years we've needed even more of this 'end of life' care. It's not a medical thing, but, to use one main example, we had someone who kept being referred back to our service: they couldn't house him; there was a lot that they couldn't do for him. He was a very vulnerable man who'd had a very tough life.

"We eventually found him more suitable accommodation; he was diagnosed with cancer a few years before. I took him to the actual scans at the hospital, to see if he could begin the treatment, then continue it. But it was all too late by this time. Then we'd help him sometimes in his personal circumstances and finally visiting, to get things washed and make sure he shaved."

"It was just to show him that we cared," Barbara interjects, "that we were not just there to fill his forms in and look after him when he came to the Centre; but we actually did *care* for him... and the fact that we would go out to visit him meant such a lot to him.

"He was always talking about watching *Sky Television,* so Gary purchased a television for him, which made a big impact on his life – even though the set wasn't that expensive. It was to show him that yes – we're still there for you – and we still care... we'll come out and support you."

"Regarding Final Years Care, during a 7-day period we'll try to visit at least once a week, but it varies: there's no one in that situation at the moment, but it's just when it arises. So we react, as things occur," she explains.

"As far as we knew this gentleman had no next-of-kin, but when we did locate someone they weren't interested. So we did all of the funeral arrangements for him and gave him a really nice, respectable send-off," Gary recalls. "We knew that he liked Elvis and the Rolling Stones. For me it was one of the highlights of the job, because it felt so worthwhile; there was a lot of satisfaction in knowing that we'd made a difference to his life.

"We also have a regular attendance of service users here at the Centre: about forty-five people on our books at any one time; we can have something between 18-26 attenders per day. Within that day we provide a range of activities to those who want that; social activities – just having someone to talk to, because disabled people can become quite isolated. It gives people a good social outlet. For people who use our services, sometimes it's the only hot meal that they get. Some people come here daily for that reason.

"But that also gives you the other side of the coin: we actually developed our kitchen services to comply with all sorts of regulations. It was expensive to do this, but it was essential, because even in 2017 there are still people who are under-nourished. They were either not eating or the food they were eating was inadequate. These are the isolated people that we're talking about," Gary continues.

"So, we start from basic need and we give one-to-one or two-to-one care according to individual need. We have two Care Suites and three toilets. A Care Suite is a bathroom for people in wheelchairs who can't do their own personal care. It's very intimate but we have to do this for adults, on a daily basis.

"They pay a small charge for our service at the Centre; we make the rest of it up with fund raising. There are local trusts all round England, for people who have pots of money, which we apply to regularly. We get a lot of refusals, but then we do have regular supporters and we try to identify new streams of funding. It's a constant job doing that.

"Government funding accounts for just a small amount, but that's connected with the Advocacy work that Barbara does. The cuts and the actual funding within Birmingham Local Authority are drastic; there are a lot of services closing.

"Fortunately for ourselves we are not solely dependent on this funding, because we do have a small charge; also, we work tirelessly on funding – we have big events – every year," explains Gary.

"We have the *Big Push* around Cannon Hill Park: going ten kilometers around the park in wheelchairs. It's proved very successful. We held it last year and this year it's on the 7th May. We're hoping there will be at least 100 people taking part.

"We advertise it through the Media, the Website, and Facebook; through Flyers and local businesses, word-of-mouth, families etc. Just trying to get it out there to as many people as we can."

"Another of our success stories," interjects Barbara, "is supporting families whose children are moving out into other accommodation; we have been instrumental in supporting five families who have moved into Supported Housing, which means that they are actual tenants. They can therefore still maintain their own benefits – their own money; which means that they can actually access the community and take up their rightful place in Society.

"They may be older parents who can no longer cope – so they have to deal with the guilt of no longer coping; they can't do what they used to do. Also, the fact that their son or daughter is moving from home.

"One particularly poignant case was a couple whose son has quite an extreme learning difficulty," she continues. "They really struggled with letting him go, but he wanted to go, so they supported him into that. He moved in and then about seven months later Mum died, so he is now able to access our service; that wouldn't have been the case if he'd gone into what's known as Traditional Residential Care, because the government are funding 24-hour care they can't then access the community."

"We have just one Residential Care Home that provides that level of care," Gary elaborates. "It's a highly under-resourced area. If you're a disabled person, it's almost impossible to live any kind of independent life. We do have a Sheltered Housing Scheme next door (mentioned earlier in the book) – Carlson Park, which sits on the land that Carlson School used to occupy. Six or seven of the people living there come here to the Centre, so transport is no problem.

"We tend to be involved with anything that happens next door; whether it's a lightbulb that goes, or something breaks, because people tend to come to us as a first call."

"Because there isn't a warden on site here," interjects Barbara, (as there was), "so everyday things can sometimes become a crisis because there no intervention there."

"Carlson House closed as a school in 1982, but it took a couple of years to close down, because there were still students there, who had to finish their education. So it would have closed over a period of time," Gary explains.

The official history of the *MSA* began when Carlson School opened in 1947, because it all developed from Carlson School, but the *Spastics Association* was officially in existence since 1963; that's when the actual Charity started. It developed because when people came out of education, including Carlson School, the biggest obstacle was that Society didn't want you when you were an adult.

"So when you got through all the legal business of being a child in Education, you had to find a job.

"But when you were a disabled person, jobs were very hard to find. And in 2018 now, they're virtually non-existent.

"We as *CPM* probably employ a higher proportion of disabled people that any other organization that I know."

Doctor Carlson's picture, one of the co-founders of Carlson House School, takes pride-of-place on the office wall; the Filkins, Cadburys and Quayles were also involved.

"This building that we're sitting in now was a shed at the end of the garden! They used to call it 'The Hut'," Gary continues.

"The school and the *MSA* were interconnected by the Walkway, as David explained in an opening chapter," adds Barbara. "You'd go through the door, into the covered walkway and then into the school... from this end. There wasn't much packing on the covered walkway, because I think the school were quite protective of their environment... and we were separate to them.

"The whole complex covered 2 acres at least – it's quite a big site," she continues. "But then when you think of the school in 1982/84, this building was built in 1960, so there'd have been a 20-year relationship there, between the school and the Centre where we are now. Even in the 1960s the people who actually came here, where we are now, were really quite able."

The Head teacher of the school married one of the porters, Barbara... Mr Brown!

"And I married the Site Manager of Bryants, David Brand, who built Carlson Park!" quips Barbara. "Gary married one of our previous managers – so no one gets away! It's just one big happy family!"

"All those years ago, staff-wise, I could be wrong about this. But when we had our daughter Nerissa, who will be fifteen at the end of February, we were the first staff couple to have children. My wife's maiden name was Sue Robbins," Gary explains.

"But there's been quite a few collaborations," he continues. "One of our support workers married one of our 'clients'; they're still happily married. If you ask anybody who comes into our service what they want out of life, the answer would be 'A relationship.' They want a partner – they want love. Sadly, there aren't many who actually achieve that."

"Again, that sets the people apart, who attended Carlson House School," adds Barbara, "because they *did* meet partners; get married.

"Carlson House was a platform to meet like-minded people who have the same problems and issues," she continues, "like Maureen and David did. Not just to do with their disability, but with their lives. And that speaks so profoundly of Carlson House School."

One of the main aims of our book is to encourage people with disabilities, albeit using David's life as the focal point of the book, to see that you can achieve things in life, despite your disability.

We realise that not everybody can lead a productive working life, so we don't want to generalize too much. We're trying to balance these two sides of the coin. What would be your view on that?

"We don't want to look at it negatively, because that will put people off," observes Barbara.

"We've worked in several specialist schools and what came about is that although we don't want to encourage negativity, we've also come across a number of young people who've got high expectations," adds Gary. "But then they realise that when they come out of education there is absolutely nothing! And we really mean *nothing*!"

"They are isolated within their families, with no expectation of work; this is at the age of nineteen when they should be at the start of their lives – fulfilling their expectations; starting on the pathway. Whereas we pick them up around 25 or 26 years of age, or later, having been at home, doing nothing; just living with Mum or Dad – or whoever," reveals Barbara.

"Society has got to realise that there is a life after nineteen for the disabled – and that should be a productive life."

So how do you cope with their depression? What can you do that's positive for them?

"We've gone around in circles, like quite a few organisations, but what do people really want: they want love; they want to have a place in the community. It's also important that they can earn money too…. Although the money isn't *everything*," comments Gary.

"What needs to be done – and I don't know how you can do it – is to make them less isolated. Because the isolation is a *massive* thing."

According to Barbara, "Gary is great: he takes two or three groups of people away on holiday every year. Because of constraints with our staffing levels it may not be possible this year. But they live for that week and they talk about it, because people haven't normally got time for them."

"The place that we use is the *Bond Hotel* in Blackpool," Gary adds. "Every room has walk-in showers. There aren't many hotels for groups of disabled people. Over the past ten years we've taken people to Belgium, Italy, and Spain; the Czech Republic; Germany and so on.

"Don't underestimate the logistics of getting ten disabled people with support staff to France! A quarter of the support staff will be volunteers. We survive here because of our flexible attitude towards work. We work weekends and evenings too. We could not run our organization without volunteers, because we are a Charity."

"The high achievers in disability are the people who step forward… make a difference – as with David – making this book," observes Barbara. "High achieving people, not just with cerebral palsy, but with any disability, they take on the mantel: they say that they want to do things for themselves – for the future – and that's great, for that section of society. But for so many people who use our services their voice is lost – they're just never going to be heard.

"But we can assure you that in the case of the 85% of people who aren't going to be able to do that and who need centres like this," she continues, "where we, at the *Association* shine, is that we try to encourage the inspiration and dreams of those who haven't got that high-achieving ability."

Gary concludes: "The majority of people who we've worked with have had happy lives; partly because of the community that we've all created together here. They want to come here; see their friends and get involved with various projects."

Chapter Twelve

My Kingdom for a Ramp!

Tina Hackett, the Physio whom you've met elsewhere in this book, explained to me, when I was fifty years old, what was happening to me. First of all, every disabled spastic person is different. Secondly, if, as an able-bodied person, you were running towards that wall, knowing that there was going to be an impact, you would brace yourself for it – and then relax.

But I can't do that: it takes me ages and ages to relax. When I go into real spasm, which hurts me, I tend to get into a vicious circle – the more it hurts, the more I go into spasm. But the more I go into spasm the more I tense up. So I have to break that sequence.

David Barnsley

Whenever I've had hospital stays in later life, all the experiences that happened to me when I was young, come back to haunt me – in spades!

At the end of this year *Motability* are renewing the lease on my vehicle, for another two years. But that was second-hand when I had it. Most people lease cars now – they don't buy them – you usually pay a deposit and then they take a proportion of the *Higher Disability Allowance*, for the maintenance of the car.

Normally I use it twice a week with Pete or Geoff; then if I need to go to the hospital, I go in my own car if I can. Jenny is unable to take the responsibility for driving me and Jane can't now, for health reasons.

I've read the books Shirley gave me – Seamus and Alton Douglas – and her new Family Saga, '65 Brunswick Road'. I'm also interested in Sport, but I tend to get tired, as the day wears on. Half the books in my bookcase I haven't read, but I've always liked books, because when I was young there was only the radio (or the Wireless as they used to call it)! I'm slow at everything and my father was very impatient. It still happens now: if people show me things in a hurry I can't remember them; I have to work them out for myself.

I'm absolutely gob-smacked by this technology – and all the rest of it. I've got a lap-top but it's not easy for me to use it. I do a bit and leave a bit... I do the best I can. I use it for my bank account – and occasionally for emails. I spent all afternoon yesterday, using the Word programme – to reply to a particular letter. I've been waiting to resolve a situation for three years, so I tried to get her to reply to that. I was editing it from a letter that I'd already written. But just as I came to the end it all disappeared! Because you have to save new documents: that's probably what went wrong!

Regarding facilities for the disabled, all buildings should be accessible for us, but they're not. Now take Lloyds Bank, Edgbaston Branch, near the university. They cannot lower the kerbstone, to enable you to get from the car park onto a path and then into the bank. It's a building that Lloyds leased from *ROSPA*; an historical building so they can't alter it.

Raj comments: "But they don't have to alter them, they can just provide a plastic ramp!"

Every shop that you go into, they still have steps. Nowadays, society seems to focus more on sport – the people who appear on television in the Paralympics and so on. Each disabled person is different, but that doesn't show up on the television or anywhere else. If you've broken your neck or back they can quantify your disability according to where you've broken it.

I've just become a trustee of the *CPA (Cerebral Palsy Midlands)* but most of the people there are not educable: they've all got mental difficulties. A lot of them are quite elderly. They're having difficulty getting referrals, because, of course, they're short of money. Birmingham City Council are withdrawing all grants.

In 2004 the Council was giving the *MSA/CPM* Grant Aid, to run the Day Centre, but now that has been drastically cut.

They've closed many of their Day Centres and Residential Homes, over a period of time. So we get people of 84 years plus coming in to the establishment where I live.

Everything's down to Finance now. In my day I never thought about who was paying for me to get this special education. Money is the root of all evil you know... And so this society is proving.

In Chapter 8, with Pete Millington's help, we compared social provision within the various eras, because certain improvements have been made.

Conversely, there are also lots of excuses as to why they haven't taken place, especially regarding steps and kerbs.

In Jane Hall's view, there have been changes in terms of adapting people's houses, to make them more Disability friendly; more access in shops, theatres and other public buildings. Although there's still room for improvement.

Shirley asked my good friend, Joe McGuire, about his experiences, regarding facilities for the disabled.

Joe explains: "Ramps and that sort of thing have improved, but regarding public buildings – usually I know where I'm going... and I know whether they are accessible or not. I normally don't visit Birmingham City Centre, but the other night, I got mixed up with a 'Blues' crowd! I was in the middle of Town at six o'clock in the evening – I didn't know where I was!"

That must have been really frightening Joe: rather like David breaking down in his Trike – in the Queensway rush-hour, of all places?!

"Well, I'd been to *Morrison's* for a meal, which is just beside the Blues Ground. I didn't realise that they were playing; it was a Cup Match," Joe continues. "When I came out I was diverted down a side road. I took the wrong turning at a roundabout and ended up in Town. It was six o'clock in the evening. The only thing I could recognise was the Rotunda, but I couldn't get to it.

"I drive a Suzuki Wagon R. Normally, I go to *Merry Hill Shopping Centre,* because it's all on the flat and it's reasonably well heated. At one time the disabled used to frequent that shopping centre. They could hire out the Power Chair. I used to see quite a lot of them, but these days, they seemed to have disappeared," observes Joe.

"I was never accustomed to going to shows like David does. But in my better days, before I was disabled, I used to go dancing! Although most of the Dance Halls have gone now," he continues.

"I remember going on holiday to the Isle of Wight; somewhere called the *County Club*. They didn't mind catering for a few disabled, but they didn't want us in large numbers, because they felt it would be off-putting for the other holidaymakers," Joe concludes.

Roger comments: "As regards transport, whereas we first had Trikes, which kept breaking down, now we have *Motability* with ordinary cars, adapted for your disability, which makes you independent. Never mind being disabled, always be cheerful – and keep smiling!"

Chapter Thirteen
On the Town Hall Steps

In 1993, the Community Care Act in Britain, changed the way in which health and social services dealt with the elderly, disabled and mentally ill (in theory providing for care at a more local level, rather than in institutions).

The following year, the film 'Forrest Gump', starring Tom Hanks, was released. Based on the novel by Winston Groom, one of its main themes was that, despite being slow-witted (a below average IQ of 75), and physically disabled, Forrest triumphs over all manner of adversity, due to his dogged determination, endearing character and devotion to duty. Like the film itself, he becomes an outstanding success.

Jane Hall repeats an earlier observation, based on experience: "There's a pressing need to re-educate the Public. In general, they are often quite rude to disabled people. Just because you're in a wheelchair doesn't mean you can't hear or can't see."

I wonder whether that's because it's an unfamiliar situation for people – and anything unknown scares them – maybe they feel out of their depth, in some cases?

"Perhaps they are," Jane responds. "Disabled children these days are more integrated into 'normal school', so other children are more used to being in the company of children in wheelchairs, or with other disabilities, so maybe their perception is better."

Integration was one of the recommendations of the Warnock Report. Carlson House closed down soon after that.

Jane comments: "If a child goes into the system with a wheelchair, or whatever his circumstances happen to be, he needs all the support he can get... that should happen."

The advantage of Carlson House was that all those facilities were made available under one roof. The pupil-staff ratios were very good. It was an ideal grounding for me Jane.

"Absolutely. It's very different nowadays; nothing much was known about disability when you were at that stage David," Jane continues. "I know you think that disabled pupils should be educated separately, but hopefully, kids these days don't discriminate so much.

"They probably think: 'oh, he's in a wheelchair – let's go and play with him.' Which is much better."

The thing about Carlson House, was that all of the pupils had some kind of disability, so that felt like the norm for them. There's an argument for both sides really, isn't there?

"Yes, but there's a world of difference between putting children with a disability into an able-bodied class, as compared to children who are severely disabled... mentally and physically: that's a very different educational situation," Jane points out. "That would require assistance from very specialised educators, to ensure that the needs of every child, and also his family, are being met."

"For somebody like yourself, David, in this day and age, to be able to integrate into normal school, would probably have been beneficial for you. Maureen would have been more difficult, because of her speech problems and so on.

"Then again, little children adapt very easily. But if we're talking about severely handicapped children, that's totally different. I don't see why a child in your circumstances, David, wouldn't be able to function in a normal school," Jane concludes.

"For a disabled person, confidence and being forthright are characteristics that, ideally, you need to have, to face the constant obstacles that are put in your way... just because of the way the general public behave... hence your choice of book title 'Against All Odds'," observes Tina.

"It's not just physical things; it's the emotional things as well. If I'm going for a hospital appointment, or for a meal, I work out where I'm going to go, how long it will take to get there. For David and Maureen you could quadruple that," Tina continues.

"Jenny made a similar point about the two of them going on holiday. Able-bodied people sometimes feel that way too. I can think of elderly relatives who've stopped doing things, because it's too difficult – but it's not really, in the grand scheme of things.

"When I started working for the *MSA*," Tina recalls, "if there was a special event like a Firework Party or whatever, my children would come as well. They became very comfortable within that environment of people with a disability. To the extent that my older daughter couldn't tell the difference between who worked at the Centre and who went there.

"So for instance, when my daughter was talking to my mother-in-law about 'Mummy's friend, Janet,' my mother-in-law would say, 'I don't think I know that friend. Who is she?' 'Oh – it's Mummy's friend who dribbles.' And she said it as she would say, 'Mummy's friend who's got a ponytail'."

Joe interjects: "The problem is that normal people don't *see* disabled people. First of all they don't realise that disabled people feel awkward... and they don't know what to talk about."

"People are not statistics, so when somebody doesn't fit the standard mould it then becomes difficult to provide the correct treatment... which applies to a lot of people with cerebral palsy," Tina observes.

"They might cover or mask it very well indeed," she continues. "I can think of one lady, who didn't appear to have any physical problems at all. She could manage around the Centre; had little jobs that were her responsibility; did various crafts – absolutely fine. Got herself to and from the bus that used to bring her. Lived with her parents; no problems at home and she did that for years and years. She'd learned a Pathway: she'd learned how to do it... the logistics of it.

"Then a group of them were invited to Birmingham Town Hall, in the 1980s – to meet the Mayor, at one of his Receptions. This lady was one of a group of six or seven who were invited to do this. I was a bit concerned about her, because I had an inkling that maybe things weren't as they appeared to be.

"When they came back they'd had a terrible time, because when she was faced with the Council House steps this lady couldn't work out how to climb them. She'd never been there before; it was quite steep. Due to the canopy and the columns she couldn't work out where the doorway was. She was in a dreadful state – and she knew that she was struggling, which made her worse. They finally got her into the Reception Room and found her a chair. Staff from the Centre were with her, so they knew her problems, but she couldn't manage.

"That was an interesting example of somebody who was fine, in their own home; their own environment. But when she was picked up and put somewhere else, those problems of Perception and Spatial Awareness returned and she had no idea where she was. When I talked to her afterwards she said: 'I can't remember the last time that happened – I thought that had stopped!' She talked about when she was a little girl and found it difficult going to places; going into shops with her mother – and things like that.

"Because she's spent so much time going backwards and forwards to the Centre; she'd got her Pattern and her little job that she did, so she could manage. That's why it's so difficult when people with those problems have to go to a hospital appointment.

"So those are the main difficulties: the increase in tone; difficulty controlling movement and Perception and Spatial Awareness," explains Tina.

"I worked within a range of deprived social conditions. One mother whose child was handicapped was asked by the owner of her local shop, not to bring her disabled child into the store, as it was upsetting the other customers. She came to me in tears: 'Where am I going to go shopping?! I've got no one to leave him with; because he's disabled no one else will look after him.'"

Mary Fletcher echoes the sentiments of several of our contributors: "People often don't see the person behind the disability. That used to apply when I went shopping with my daughter (not so much now).

"When we came to pay for something, they would give the change to my daughter – and she'd say, 'No, it's not for me, it's for Mum'."

John Fletcher interjects: "Yes, they've also asked our daughter, what her mother would like, and she replied, 'Ask her!'"

"But the thing is," Mary continues, "the people asking us were embarrassed because they only saw our disability. It sometimes helps if disabled people will talk to them more, to put them at their ease.

"Dave, Maureen, John and myself have always been disabled, so that's just normal for us: it's always been part of our lives. As an able-bodied person, you could miss out on that side of life too – if you didn't want to be bothered.

"It isn't all about Disability," Mary continues. "It's about being determined to do what you want to do, whether you're able-bodied or not. Disabled people also need to be aware that they are different in some ways, although they don't always want to feel that they are... so they sometimes have to put the person at ease.

"When people have asked 'what's the matter with you,' I just say, 'Well, I just can't walk as well as you. But I'm all right really. It's just something in my brain that isn't quite right. It's like a computer chip: in my case it just doesn't work properly.'"

Sadly Mary, I've noticed, when I've visited various clubs for the disabled, in more recent years, the degree of the disability seems to be worse than in my youth. I attribute this to Political Correctness, Anti-abortion Campaigns and so on. The birth has to be allowed to go ahead, even though the child may have a severely disabled life ahead of him.

Raj comments: "They're not given enough chances are they? You know how Black and Asian people are still struggling to get into Media, films and programmes – and when they do, they get stereo-typed? If the Disabled person gets a part, the focus is on their disability; if a black man gets a part, it's usually based on his colour.

"One solution might be to have Special Needs Schools and Mainstream Schools, running side-by-side, so the lessons are different but the playground is the same," she suggests.

"Mainstream school integration can work with mental disabilities, like autism, but it's not working with physical disabilities, because the buildings aren't always suitable. Why are the Special Needs Schools several miles away? Why can every other mother take her child, kiss him at the gate and say good-bye? But if you've got a disabled child, they've got to be bussed to school.

"If able-bodied people saw disabled children, from an early age it wouldn't seem abnormal. My child doesn't ask why David's in a wheelchair. Joe came into the room while my children were there. They didn't ask me why he was in a wheelchair. They just accepted it, because they're young. I don't say, "Let's go and see my disabled friend David," I just say, "Let's go and see David," Raj concludes.

Mary has experienced situations where 'Lip Service' is paid to the subject.

"We live in quite an old town, in Tamworth, and a lot of the buildings are listed; because of that, they can't alter them," she explains.

"That can be difficult. We have a local pub that serves really nice food, but we can't get in, because there's a step. They can't alter it, because it's a listed building. There are quite a few like that – and it can be really annoying. Some rules aren't worth the paper they're written on!

"Who wants to use the gardens in the summertime, when you can't go in the winter? (although we have been known to do that!) A lot of the gardens are better; some of them have level access, which is quite good, but then you've got heavy doors to open! It's a real nightmare, when you're trying to wheel yourself, open the door, and wedge yourself against the door – making sure it doesn't shut on you, as you leave!" Mary concludes.

I've made a special request about what I want at my own funeral (but let's hope that's not going to happen any time soon!)

Jenny explains: "Yes, David's very adamant that he does not want anyone to stand up to sing or pray. He just feels it's a great equalizer if we do it that way."

Shirley had a taste of 'levelling the playing field', when she was a Games Teacher. She spent time with paraplegic members of a basketball team at the Victoria School in Northfield. They were actually the Area Champions. In order to join in with them she was obliged to play basketball from a wheelchair: propelling it with one hand and shooting goals from a seated position. It played havoc with her back and shoulder muscles, but it was the only way to function, by operating under the same conditions. It gave her a glimpse of what it must be like to be permanently disabled.

Jenny continues: "In Dave's case especially, because he worked for *Lucas's* for twenty-eight years, (awarded a certificate after 25 years' service)... he had to get up every morning. It was a struggle: he was sick every morning, before he set out."

Roger observes: "I admire people who were once able-bodied, but then maybe an accident happens; perhaps lose a limb, then realise what it's like to be disabled. That applies to Joe, because a tumour suddenly developed on his spine. There was also a very intelligent chap, who used to go to the Club, but he had a motorbike accident, resulting in brain damage… cerebral palsy. But as I often say, 'There's always someone worse than yourself.'

"If you are unable to do something or need assistance, always ask, so I think things have improved for Disabled people. But there's discrimination when they say things like, 'Oh, you can't come on the bus with that chair!'" Roger continues.

"People will tell me that they've got a Disabled toilet and I'll ask, 'Oh, is the seat burnt?' That's my humour. At the Woodlands I got to the toilet, but I couldn't get out. All they need to do is have a two-way door – problem solved. They've got a Disabled Toilet at *Tesco's* with a door that you can open both ways, so you don't get stuck. Things have improved for Disabled people," Roger concludes, "although sometimes you get people saying, 'Oh, I wouldn't like to be like that!'"

According to Pete Millington: "Due to less efficient services people are feeling more isolated. In Birmingham alone, the City has got this massive deficit, so the money isn't there to meet the needs.

"People have to employ their own solicitor now," he continues, "with Legal Aid no longer available – well who's going to be able to do that?! On the other hand, a lot has changed for the better. At least wheelchair users can get on and off buses and trains now; a lot of public buildings are better, but take the new library, for example. Millions of pounds have been spent on it. It's largely accessible, but there are tiny little bits, where the lifts don't go up high enough, so there are big queues for them."

Shirley directs Pete's attention to a series of articles in the *Telegraph Magazine*, about mothers who have Downs Syndrome babies, but they'd all kept their babies. Although this only represents the point of view of three particular women, their children have turned out to be so wonderful and special. Everybody's an individual and just because they have a disability doesn't mean they're not worthwhile human beings.

"Absolutely! I go into Day Centres, such as the one in Sutton Coldfield, for Autism and I absolutely love it," observes Pete. "Not in a patronizing way, but the challenges that those people as individuals present, because each group is so diverse – and the humour and insight – you can never ever make assumptions about anyone.

"I'll give you just one example: we teach people about personal safety, so we do a session about Safety in the Home. I was delivering this course to a group of people with Autism. I try to involve them as well, so I say, 'Can everyone think of a danger in the kitchen, such as a chip pan et cetera?'

"I came to this one guy, who'd never talked before; he was just silent and perplexed. So I passed on, because I didn't want to embarrass him, by hanging on there. The lesson continued, with me thinking that the guy was there to make up the numbers, which is fine – he's here for social reasons.

"Then at the end of the session, he came up to me; he stood about two inches away from me, with really focused eye contact, while he repeated the whole lesson to me, point by point... it was amazing!

"I went back to the same group, about a year later. The students had changed, apart from this one guy, who was still there. He was about twenty-two. I asked him if he remembered anything about that lesson, twelve months previously. And he repeated it in the same sequenced detail – just as he had done before! I thought: 'right, I'm never going to pre-judge a situation like that, ever again!'"

As a teacher, Shirley found that even with children who appeared to be dysfunctional, if you can find something that they're particularly interested in, you can totally transform the situation.

"Maybe that's what we're not doing in society?" questions Pete. "Especially with people who just have a physical impairment. We're not using their talents to the full."

Chapter Fourteen
End Game

My parents first taught me to play chess as an eight-year-old – and my enthusiasm for the game has remained with me, throughout my life. The title of this chapter is therefore, particularly apt, as it includes ways in which I've been trying to cope with disability, in later life.

David Barnsley

Fellow enthusiasts, Chris Evans and Peter Hughes, belong to a local Birmingham club, the *Mutual Chess Club*, which meets at the *Stadium*, Wheelers Lane. These two friends of mine continue to challenge me, regularly, to a game or two, at my apartment.

A typical day, for me, would be as follows:

At seven o'clock my alarm goes off and I try to come round, by taking off the mask, which I've worn throughout the night. I feel pretty bad – to be honest with you, as I try to breathe normally, without the support of the mask and the air blowing onto my face. I always put my mask on myself, at night.

0.5% of it is oxygen, but the rest is just non-invasive (NVA) air going on to my face. As I switch that off I'm starting to breathe normally, but I feel absolutely dried-up. Although I have a humidifier on the back, it seems, recently, that all of the water drains out, during the night.

I can't see clearly until I've had a drink of water and taken my tablets – I prepare those myself. They're in a Blister Pack. But when I open my eyes, it's a blur! I put the television on – to try to focus on the time. When I've drunk some water, wind comes out of almost every orifice. That's why I can't take the iron tablets that I'm supposed to!

I try to drink a pint of water, before I'm fully awake. I cannot do virtually *anything* for myself, now, because any effort that I make affects my breathing; I'm told that I'm taking in too much carbon monoxide.

I'm thinking fairly clearly, straight away really – after I've got the water in.

David's chess partners: from l-r: Chris Evans, with his partner, Jan; Peter Hughes, Joan Flanagan and her friend, (with her back to the camera).

The Care Staff come in for 8.30am, so I've been lying there, trying to pull myself round, for an hour-and-a-half. They then give me a Bed Bath and help me get dressed. There have to be two staff – and they do that every single morning.

It usually takes about fifty minutes to hoist me out of bed and into my chair – and get me dressed in a reasonable style. Then into the kitchen, where I brush my teeth before I eat (much against my better judgement) followed by breakfast, which is a fairly substantial one, because my breathing is best at that time and swallowing is a problem: I have 'Barretts Oesophagus', which makes it difficult to eat.

My thoughts are at their *clearest* when I wake up around three or four o'clock in the morning: that is my best thinking time.

I try to achieve something – no matter how small it may appear to anyone else – every day.

As I wake up in the morning, foremost in my mind is how I'm going to get through the day. I have a fairly routine sort of week.

Some things give me satisfaction, but other days I feel quite suicidal.

This is the way I feel, because having been brought up from a very early age, to do as much as I can for myself – and be independent (although I have never been truly independent and I would question whether anybody is independent) – you always need other people. And I've found this considerably difficult.

At school we were taught: 'If at first you don't succeed, try, try, try again'. So I *have* done; the fact that it takes me longer to do things than anybody else has always been a huge stumbling block for me. In early years I was supposed to spend time relaxing, lying on the floor, et cetera.

I shave myself around 9.20am and I won't see the Care Staff again, until just before I'm going to go out, when I check my catheter, to make sure it's empty. I have frequent drinks to keep me hydrated, including a cranberry and orange drink, to prevent urinary problems.

I'm finally ready to face the world at about half past ten.

I'm fortunate, at the moment, to have the support of Jenny, Jane and Joan.

They shop for all of my meals and daily needs. This morning I had a bacon and tomato sandwich. I don't have cereal because it's not substantial enough for the tablet I have to take, for my bowels. My stomach is a big problem: I have a huge hiatus hernia. It blocks out everything: I've had endoscopes and goodness-knows-what!

I used to go out to choose my own food, with Jane, but I haven't done that now, for some time. When possible, I visit the Farm Shop in Studley, to get my eggs.

Jenny, Jane or Joan will take care of Lunch and Tea, except for two days a week, which is Tuesday and Friday, when the Care Staff are supposed to help me get some food; but they're used to coming in and having very little to do.

People say that my flat always looks neat and tidy – but it has to be, because I'll be lying on my back, staring at the ceiling, while the Care Staff ask me where everything is! They have regular training sessions, but the capability of individual staff members varies.

They come to give me my Lunch Call after two o'clock. But I never relax – I'm on the go, all the time. When I'm eating I'm trying to get the food down, but I don't really want it! And I'm preoccupied with my bowels, most of the time, which tend to run in sequence: either I can't go or I'm going too much! It gets me down, because when I want to go to the toilet, I have to wait until they've got time to put me on it… sometimes it's too late!

So there are positives and the negatives to all of this.

My Carers are supposed to do my tea as well, but I usually ask Jenny to help me with that. The sort of thing that I have is Prawn Salad, or some other salad with brown bread and butter. I've not supposed to have too much brown bread and butter, but I've eaten it all my life, so I'm not going to stop now! I have that about half past five.

Unfortunately, like any Extra Care Development, the attitudes of staff can vary considerably. One morning a week I have mushrooms on toast. Every time,

David's 75th Birthday Party. From l-r: Salim, Aisha and Fatma.

one particular Carer asks me how to do it! And she's an extremely difficult person to get on with.

Sadly, there was also an incident where I was hit by one of the Carers – Police and Health & Safety had to be notified... but that's an exception.

The best Carers here tend to be the Asians. Personally, I didn't want a male Carer in my life, because all of my previous Carers, nurses et cetera, Mummy and my aunts, were all women.

But we were told that Salim was coming, so I gave him the benefit of the doubt. He, Aisha, Abdul and Rabina, amongst others, are part of a team who have turned out to be very good and caring Carers.

My mind is always ahead of my ability, so there is frustration in that. But as the day wears on, I get more tensed up and more tired.

My mother understood that I mustn't be rushed: as soon as you try to rush me I tend to freeze. I also find the fact that I can't keep up with able-bodied people very frustrating. So I try to get round that by being well prepared – and remain as relaxed as I possibly can... which is part of the waking up and getting up procedure really.

I very much appreciate the help given to me, by both the Day and Night Nurses... two separate teams. The Day Nurses (or 'Gods-on-Wheels', as I call them!) work under the leadership of Marie. The Night Nurses are there to provide help, should I need it. The combined help of these two teams of nurses, is what keeps me going!

My Consultant Respiratory Physician, at The Queen Elizabeth Hospital, is Doctor Shyam Madathil. He and his nurses, Jody, Theresa and Lyndsey, are also keeping me alive!

Shirley and I have been leafing through my old autograph book. Some of the signatures include Harry Oakes (Dan Archer); Robert Mawdesley, (Walter Gabriel); Roy Rogers (when he came to my Harborne school: someone got that for me, as I wasn't there at the time).

Moving through the book, dating from my childhood onwards, I've got Professor Jimmy Edwards; E. Collins who was a master at Carlson School: it's the entry that says 'My mother always told me that if I kept trying my name I would be on the BBC. Best of luck forever.'

Then we've got Ronnie Hanbury, the scriptwriter for the BBC. The ventriloquist, Bill Worsley; the Fraser House Quartet (one of them was married to Beryl Reed); Cardew, 'The Cad' Robinson; Jewel & Warriss, comedians; Kay Cavendish, the actress; Jack Warner (Dixon of Dock Green).

I've also got signatures of the Birmingham City Football Cup Team 1956: Noel Kingsley; Arthur Turner the manager; Eddie Brown; Len Boyd; Geoff Hall (he died of polio). The team came to Carlson House in 1956, so that's why I've got the signatures.

I'm possibly unique, from the point of view of relishing Carlson House as the foundation upon which I built my life. But if there's any former pupil out there who feels the same way – do let me know!

As our 'End Game' draws towards its close, we've asked some of my friends and acquaintances to provide insights into my true nature.

"I've known David for such a long time," begins Joe – "since 1969 – almost 50 years! I would say that he's pretty generous by nature. Many a meal I've had – whether it was in Solihull or elsewhere.

"But he's a chap who has had to manage for himself a lot," he continues. "So consequently he's usually thinking of how to manage for himself – and how things affect him.

"Possibly that was reinforced by his upbringing. He's also competitive. Say, for example, that you're going on a trip and you were leading at the front, the next time he'd want to be leading the line of cars," Joe continues.

"He has to have something to keep his mind at ease – a project – like this book now – and holidays – that sort of thing. He's been far more adventurous than me; going on holidays and taking the electric chair with him. And going with Maureen to various places. The Hawaiian holiday was particularly ambitious."

"Although he doesn't like the word, I think Dave is very brave," Jenny remarks. "He can be an 'Old Git' at times, but I don't know if I could have done what he did. It takes a lot of courage and a lot of determination, to get up every day.

"He's also bloody stubborn – and he always wants a project; he'll do something – then wish he hadn't. He loves his holidays, but then the day before he's going, 'I don't want to go!'"

"It's because it's such an effort – even to the height of the bed; the height of the toilet. This was before he was hoisted. Everything. After Maureen's death, when he was travelling on his own, because I know him, when he said he didn't want to go I'd say 'Well don't then.' Then he'll reply: 'I've got to go now. I've said I will.' However, if he says he's going to do something, he will do it. He won't let anyone down. It's that determination that's got him through isn't it? He's always had that stubborn streak," Jenny continues.

"He's also a very generous person… to his own detriment, at times. People have used him and abused that generosity. He trusts everyone, until they hurt him – and there have been some horrible people!"

"He's given up now, with holidays," she continues. "But to have that impetus to do it at all, the logistics of the wheelchairs and transport! Just horrendous. I think I would have given up years ago."

Jenny's husband, Pete, comments: "It's very difficult, because sometimes he appears very lonely – everybody's against him: the care staff. So I try to be positive with him, if he's negative."

"Try reverse psychology with him – it works every time!" Jenny interjects.

"When something goes wrong for him that's it – it's set in stone then… like when the batteries on his wheelchair went: 'I'm never going to leave this room again!' I say, 'Dave you will… Plan B.'"

"The thing is that we can see his wheelchair, but he can't – it's underneath him. So when this happened about the batteries I went and got his other wheelchair," Pete explains. "I got the chair out of the store-room. It was charged up and we had to get Gwen, one of the care staff in, to get him out of the one that needed recharging. The spare one is more difficult to operate, because it's not set for his leg positions."

Jenny elaborates: "The other chair, which he could have used, which we're calling Plan B, he wouldn't do it, because Plan A wasn't working. So he was sat in Plan A wheelchair for three days before he thought: "Well, I'll give Plan B a go.""

"As he'd had different problems with wheelchairs, I found a place in Halesowen and Rugeley," Pete continues. "He said, 'They're not open for Wednesday.' 'But I can go on the Internet, find these batteries and go and get them Dave!'

"The objective of getting it done right away wasn't important to him, because he know that *particular* man from up North will come and fix his chair. And he thinks the world of people who help him like that: he really does appreciate them. It's the same with the nurses who fix his mask."

Pete Willock, David's trusty driver – to many destinations. Photo taken at St Andrews, as part of his 70th birthday celebrations. Pete had the honour of presenting the match ball to the referee, before the home match, between Birmingham City and Newcastle United. Photographer: Max Spielmann Studio.

I'm a great one for thanking the people who've been important in my life Pete… and there's something to be said for using the 'tried-and-tested' methods, rather than something different – which might go wrong!

"He says, 'I was well, 'til they made me better!'" Pete remarks. "It's the same with his Dad: he made him do things, even though sometimes it felt like bullying."

"His Dad used to say, 'You'll never drive a car. You'll never get married,' as a challenge to him," Jenny interjects.

"Dave's very proud of what he's done, even though he doesn't boast about it. And sometimes he's very jealous," Pete observes. "He likes to be the centre of attention, so if there's a group of you, he must be the focus. So when I've been out helping him or driving him, or whatever, and we meet up with other people, if I'm laughing and joking with those other people, he doesn't like it. Sometimes, when we're out in the car I say, 'If you misbehave I'll slam these brakes on so hard, you'll be in front of me!' And he just has a bit of a chuckle. And when we come back from our Mystery Tours, he always thanks me. So in that closed envelope of two blokes he's probably more appreciative than he is when he's in the flat, with Jane and Jen.

"Did he tell you about his 75th Birthday party?" Pete continues. "Joe had already had *his* 75th party at the Home and he hired one of these Irish singers – 'Little Jimmy'. So Dave just booked him again, out of the blue… Jenny and Jane made a party for him."

Jenny explains: "Earlier in the year, a few months before his birthday, Dave said, 'I'm surprised you're not nagging me!' But once I heard that, Jane and I just went ahead and organized it, because that's a sort of *code* for the fact that he would like you to!"

"Barbara Brand came to the party, with her husband," Pete elaborates. "I've still got some photos of Dave, going on the Flying Scotsman, last September. If he's in a happy mood, he can be the best company; if he's in Mr Grumpy mode then you've got to be tough with him – and bring him back on side.

"There can be times when we arrive where we have to pick up the pieces. He may have had a disaster with the care staff, because they haven't got him up on time, so he'll then think that everything else is going to go wrong that day. You've come in to that situation – so you get the negativity out of him – and put him back on track."

"It's got to the stage now, where he knows us so well, if you say to him, 'Oh Dave, what a *shame* – what *are* we going to do?!' He'll say, 'Are you being sarcastic or what?'" Jenny concludes.

According to Tina, "The first word that comes to mind is 'Strength'. David has a very strong personality; very confident; sometimes 'bolshie'; very forthright.

"Some people have suggested that he is very focused on himself – and if you mention anything about yourself, it quickly comes back round to him. But that's

David celebrates his 75th birthday: from l-r, back row: Jane Hall, Jenny Willock and Barbara Humpage. Photographer: Pete Willock.

just a form of early conditioning – not something that I would particularly focus on. Because if I think of all the children and adults that I've worked with, (the vast majority of those have had cerebral palsy)… they *all* feel like that. So it's nothing out of the ordinary really," Tina observes.

"We went for a wheelchair appointment. David was hoping to have a new version of the same chair that he already had. The Consultant, who seemed otherwise quite experienced, wanted to explain to the students a little bit about David and about why he was there; the sort of chair he was in and why. But because of Political Correctness, and the procedure he was expected to follow, he was trying very hard not to say the word 'spastic'! He was going round and round in circles. The expression on the students' faces was saying: we've no idea what you're talking about! They were also whispering to each other. In fact, it was creating the very problem that they were trying to avoid!

"I could see David getting more and more 'hot under the collar' and more exasperated," Tina recalls. "Eventually he leant forward, walloped the desk with his hand, and shouted: 'Why don't you say it? I'm a Spastic; I've always been a Spastic; I'll always be a Spastic – that's the problem – I'm a Spastic!!'

"The look of shock, horror and incredulity on the Consultant's face! But suddenly the students understood the situation," observes Tina. "Presumably they also understood why their Consultant, who was normally very coherent, had been behaving that way! You could almost see him decide: right – we'd better carry on then.

"He straightened his collar and coat and went: 'You can see, Mr Barnsley is a very forthright gentleman!' And on they went. But that was where we were – at that time," Tina concludes.

Roger Robinson and I have complementary personalities: he's more 'laid back', and I'm more intense.

"That's fair, although at the same time, David was well-educated, but he's changed so much over the years," observes Roger. "His mobility has worsened in the last few years: he has breathing difficulties.

"Myself, I don't like this part of my life where I'm unable to do what I used to do. But this is life, so you'd better take it with a pinch of salt – and just get on with it!

"I'm still able to drive my car," Roger continues, "but it's more difficult getting in and out. I can't walk too well now, so I use a wheelchair, but I've always got friends; my sons and daughters; friends at my club. I enjoy myself that way.

"I have three children, but their Mum, Jenny, passed away. I've got two girls and a boy – Karen, Lisa and Simon. I've also got grandchildren and great grandchildren. That's the difference between myself and David (not being nasty or anything). I've got a really good family, whereas David is on his own in that respect."

Tina observes: "Many people with CP have difficulty with Perception and/or Spatial Awareness, but David has few problems in that respect."

That's one of the main themes of our book, Tina: unless you're severely disabled, you can achieve a lot. So do whatever you can.

According to John Fletcher: "David is a tremendous chap. He has a most marvellous memory – and he can come back with things that happened sixty years ago! He can talk to you about things and get you tied up in knots!

"He's very interested in steam trains, cars – anything involving history. He can talk about all of that – he's marvellous! On the negative side, I don't want to lose a friend – but David can be very outspoken, at times; if there's anything he doesn't agree with, he will certainly tell you... and explain to you why."

"On the positive side I can only say what John has said – and to be able to be here, living on his own, having gone through the traumas that he has, I think he's absolutely wonderful! I know he wouldn't think that himself, but I think he's done really well, over the years, to get where he is now, at the age that he is," observes Mary.

"On the negative side, he's very outspoken. I've known him for a long time and he's said that I've upset him on numerous occasions, but I wouldn't do that for the world! I think the fact that he's outspoken is because of the frustration with not being able to do things himself: that doesn't help him, because he wants something done, that he can't physically do," Mary continues.

"Dave can do these things mentally, and this is the most frustrating part, that physically, he finds it almost impossible. But he will give you instructions about how to do it," adds John.

"At the moment, we're a little bit more able and can do a bit more," interjects Mary. "I can walk, but also use a wheelchair. David isn't able to do that anymore."

Raj describes David as "... kind and considerate; he thinks about people around him; he always wants to make somebody else comfortable."

According to his school report, David was like that from an early age.

"He will help in any way: foolishly, even if it means that he's at a loss, he will try and help you, if he can," Raj continues. "So he's positive and if you go to David with a problem, he's full of knowledge – he always has constructive suggestions to make. He's an intelligent bloke: he knows everything about everything.

"I would phone him sometimes to ask him what things mean. When I first met them they'd use big bloody words and I'd have to go home and look them up in a dictionary! But yes – he'd always try to help you out.

"On the negative side, he *can* come across as very arrogant at times – and sometimes he doesn't respect people's privacy. He's quite happy to talk about people's business to other people.

"The good thing about various issues that David and I have had is that it raised our relationship to a different level of understanding. But Maureen and David made me feel that I was at home. They made me feel part of them. Hence our friendship – to this day," Raj concludes.

It has to be said that *some* disabled people are very snappy when kind people offer them help. Whereas when people offer me help, and I can manage without it, I say: "Thank you very much for the thought, but I'm all right." They can be very rude to the able-bodied section of society, and I really feel that they do us down, when they're trying to improve life for disabled people.

On the same subject, Tina draws our book to a close, with one of her own experiences:

"My children would be about two and six. We were in a very crowded pub, on holiday, having a meal. A group of people came in on a coach trip – several in wheelchairs; several unsteady; several with walking sticks. We ended up sitting next to a lady, who looked as if the last place on earth she wanted to be was on this coach trip. She was in a wheelchair, she had a face like thunder and she was snapping at everybody.

"The poor chap who wheeled her in was obviously getting a mouthful-and-a-half! They ended up sitting next to us. I noticed my one daughter staring at this lady – looking her up and down – and at the wheelchair… and going all the way round it.

"My daughter was six years old and I remember thinking: 'I wonder what's going to happen here?!' Suddenly, I realised that this lady was also watching my daughter. The face like thunder didn't change and I thought: 'Oh dear – something's going to happen in a minute!'" Tina continues.

"Suddenly, my daughter said to her, 'Don't your legs work?!' And I thought: 'This could go one of two ways!'

"The woman looked at her – and a smile just spread across her face. She said, 'No, my legs don't work very well at all!' My daughter said, 'It's good you've got some wheels then!' The lady grinned and said, 'Do you want to have a look?'

"And for the next twenty minutes, while everyone else was trying to organise food for this little group, there was this same lady, whose face had *completely* changed, explaining how the brakes worked, how the wheels worked; the bag on the back; the footplate! She worked the brakes.

"Then this poor guy, who'd had such a hard time, came back; stood there with her plate of food, thinking, 'What on earth's going on here?!'

"So the situation completely changed. The mood of the whole place changed… simply because this little girl had said, 'Don't your legs work?'

"It made me wonder what this lady had encountered before: had she been someone who'd had complaints because her wheelchair was in the way? People not being friendly? Talking to her Carer and not to her? And this little girl had just lifted the moment.

"People can be open and see the person behind the disability," concludes Tina. "If *somehow* that attitude could become more widespread…"

Appendices

1. Sir Ludwig Guttmann – a Short Biography

(3 July 1899 – 18 March 1980)

Sir Ludwig 'Poppa' Guttmann, a German-born, British neurologist, established the Paralympic Games in England. A Jewish doctor, he fled Germany, just before the outbreak of World War Two, having already established himself as Germany's top neurosurgeon, by 1933.

He was to become one of the founding fathers of organized physical activities for the Disabled.

Having settled in Oxford, England, in 1939, he continued his research into spinal injury, at the Nuffield Department of Neurosurgery, in the Radcliffe Infirmary. As a result of the displacement of academic Jews from Europe, the Jewish Community in Oxford grew rapidly. Sir Ludwig's daughter, Eva became friendly with Miriam Margolyes, now a famous actress.

Guttmann subsequently developed Stoke Mandeville Stadium, the UK National Centre for Disability Sport, in conjunction with his work at the hospital.

In August 2012 the BBC broadcast a film, *The Best of Men*, about Guttmann's work at Stoke Mandeville Hospital (see also our Bibliography).

He was awarded an OBE in the 1950 King's Birthday Honours List, followed later by a CBE; in 1966, he received a knighthood from Queen Elizabeth II.

His pioneering work and his firm belief that sport was a major therapy for helping injured military personnel to build up physical strength and self-respect, has vastly improved medical help for countless disabled people, leaving a lasting legacy, in terms of their medical treatment.

2. Beatitudes for the Disabled

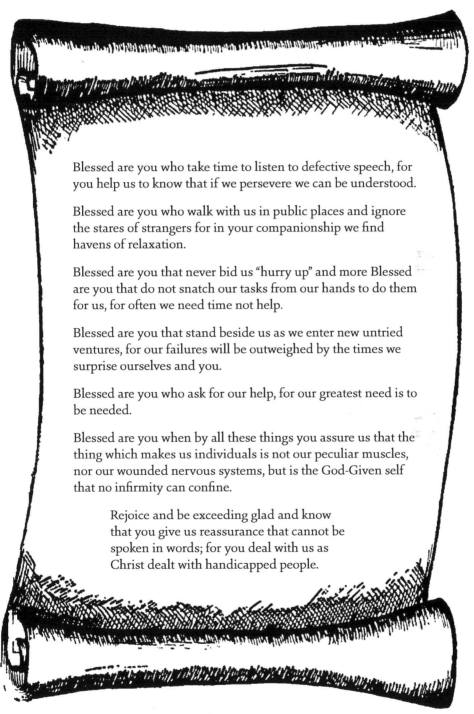

Blessed are you who take time to listen to defective speech, for you help us to know that if we persevere we can be understood.

Blessed are you who walk with us in public places and ignore the stares of strangers for in your companionship we find havens of relaxation.

Blessed are you that never bid us "hurry up" and more Blessed are you that do not snatch our tasks from our hands to do them for us, for often we need time not help.

Blessed are you that stand beside us as we enter new untried ventures, for our failures will be outweighed by the times we surprise ourselves and you.

Blessed are you who ask for our help, for our greatest need is to be needed.

Blessed are you when by all these things you assure us that the thing which makes us individuals is not our peculiar muscles, nor our wounded nervous systems, but is the God-Given self that no infirmity can confine.

> Rejoice and be exceeding glad and know
> that you give us reassurance that cannot be
> spoken in words; for you deal with us as
> Christ dealt with handicapped people.

3. Certificate and Photograph from Event Commemorating 25 Years Service at Lucas

Presented by the Directors to

DAVID BARNSLEY

as a mark of
appreciation & goodwill
upon completing

25 YEARS

loyal & efficient service with

LUCAS

Godfrey Messervy

Chairman
October 1984

Select Bibliography

Articles:

Archives about the Warnock Report (see also websites)

Looking Into the Eighties – David Barnsley, published in the MSA Annual Book, 1980, for Fundraising purposes.

An Interview with David Barnsley – 2-part series of short biographical Articles, by Peter Millington.

Books:

A History of the Cadbury Trust – Merlin Waterson and Samantha Wyndham, Published by the Barrow Cadbury Trust, 2013.

An Introduction to Invalid Carriages – Stuart Cyphus. Published by the Author 2006.

Forward – The History of Birmingham Disability Resource Centre, by Pete Millington and Hazel Wood. Published by Birmingham Disability Resource Centre 2010. Lottery funded.

Fulfilment Through Achievement – the History of Cerebral Palsy Midlands, and its Community of People 1947 – 2014; author, Charlotte Clark; 2nd Edition: edited by Sandra Rowan, Celia Noble, Allyson and Sarah Lilly, Gary Watson and Zac Loftus. Published by CPM.

Films/Documentaries:

Steps to Independence – made by Brian Filkin, as a fund-raising project for the MSA.

The Best of Men – BBC television film about Ludwig Guttmann's work at Stoke Mandeville Hospital, during and after the Second World War. First broadcast August 2012, with Eddie Marsan as Dr. Guttmann and Rob Brydon as one of the seriously injured patients, given a purpose in life by the doctor.

Documents:

David's Carlson House School Report, July 1959.

Magazines and Periodicals:
Sunday Telegraph article about mothers who continue to care for their handicapped babies, with heartwarming results, 2017.

Newspapers:
Birmingham Post and Mail article: *Holiday for Three by Invalid Car* – (name and date of Staff reporter unavailable); 1961.
Obituaries: a) Jessie Barnsley, May 1996; b) Maureen Barnsley, September 2000.

Websites:
CPM; MSA; Disability Resource Centre. Wikipedia: range of information, including Baroness Warnock and the Warnock Report. Also, Ludwig Guttmann.

By the Same Author

All the above titles are available to purchase at www.brewinbooks.com